Fairy Quest

Outlaws

Jenkins • Ramos • Olea

BOOM!
STUDIOS™

ROSS RICHIE CEO & Founder • **MATT GAGNON** Editor-in-Chief • **FILIP SABLIK** VP-Publishing & Marketing • **LANCE KREITER** VP-Licensing & Merchandising • **PHIL BARBARO** Director of Finance • **BRYCE CARLSON** Managing Editor
DAFNA PLEBAN Editor • **SHANNON WATTERS** Editor • **ERIC HARBURN** Editor • **CHRIS ROSA** Assistant Editor • **ALEX GALER** Assistant Editor • **WHITNEY LEOPARD** Assistant Editor • **JASMINE AMIRI** Assistant Editor
STEPHANIE GONZAGA Graphic Designer • **MIKE LOPEZ** Production Designer • **DEVIN FUNCHES** E-Commerce & Inventory Coordinator • **BRIANNA HART** Executive Assistant • **AARON FERRARA** Operations Assistant

FAIRY QUEST Volume One — December 2013. Published by BOOM! Studios, a division of Boom Entertainment, Inc. Fairy Quest is Copyright © 2013 ClockStop Entertainment, Inc. All rights reserved.
BOOM! Studios™ and the BOOM! Studios logo are trademarks of Boom Entertainment, Inc., registered in various countries and categories. All characters, events, and institutions depicted herein are fictional.
Any similarity between any of the names, characters, persons, events, and/or institutions in this publication to actual names, characters, and persons, whether living or dead, events, and/or institutions is
unintended and purely coincidental. BOOM! Studios does not read or accept unsolicited submissions of ideas, stories, or artwork.

A catalog record of this book is available from OCLC and from the BOOM! Studios website, www.boom-studios.com, on the Librarians page.

BOOM! Studios, 5670 Wilshire Boulevard, Suite 450, Los Angeles, CA 90036-5679. Printed in Singapore. First Printing. ISBN: 978-1-60886-345-7

STORY
Paul Jenkins

ART
Humberto Ramos

COLOR ART, DESIGN & LETTERING
Leonardo Olea

COVER
Humberto Ramos
with Leonardo Olea

LOGO DESIGN
Adriana Soria

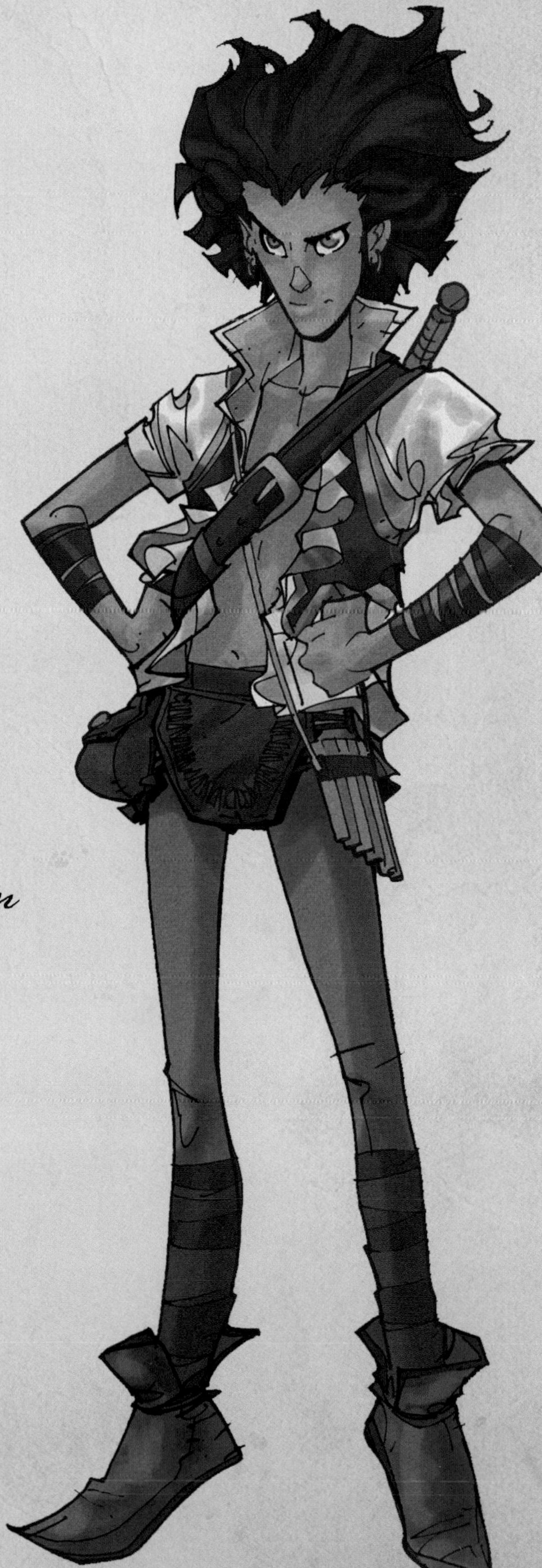

BOOM! STUDIOS EDITION

ASSISTANT EDITOR
Alex Galer

EDITOR
Bryce Carlson

TRADE DESIGNER
Hannah Nance Partlow

Special Thanks

For my dream girl, my nigh perfect wife, Melinda, who gets more beautiful every day.

For my little guys, Jack and Billy, who love to share new dreams with their Daddy.

For my friends Karen Berger, Lou Stathis and Kevin Eastman, who taught me how to explain my dreams.

For my genius friend, Humberto, who makes the dream come to life, and for our genius pal, Leo, who gives it shape.

—Paul

This book is dedicated to all of you who dared to have a dream and followed no matter what.

To all the people who gave me a little of their precious time and a lot of wisdom.

To the Spacemonkeys and D'artagnan whose friendship and love means a world of joy and happiness.

To Jenkins who believed in the "kid" from south of the border.

So, spread yourselves with pixie dust and follow me to the second star to the right, and straight 'til morning...

The journey is about to begin.

—Humberto

The journey is about to begin...

Memorable characters always have a fulfilling story to tell. I happen to live, enjoy and work with the best characters that can be found in the "Realworld": Thanks to Humberto for letting me carry this baby and change its diapers (believe me, you can enjoy that).

Thanks to Paul for having me entertained making his words fly through every page.

Thanks to all the great artists for their true love with their pin-ups.

Thanks to Olea Creative's warriors: Juan Farjado for his hard work (he loves the pages with rain), Alicia Ortiz for her very meticulous work and Irma for her amazing cooking.

And thanks to you, for giving us the chance to tell you this particular secret story before going to bed.

Until then, wake up, is time to deviate.

—Olea

Don't believe what
the storybooks say...

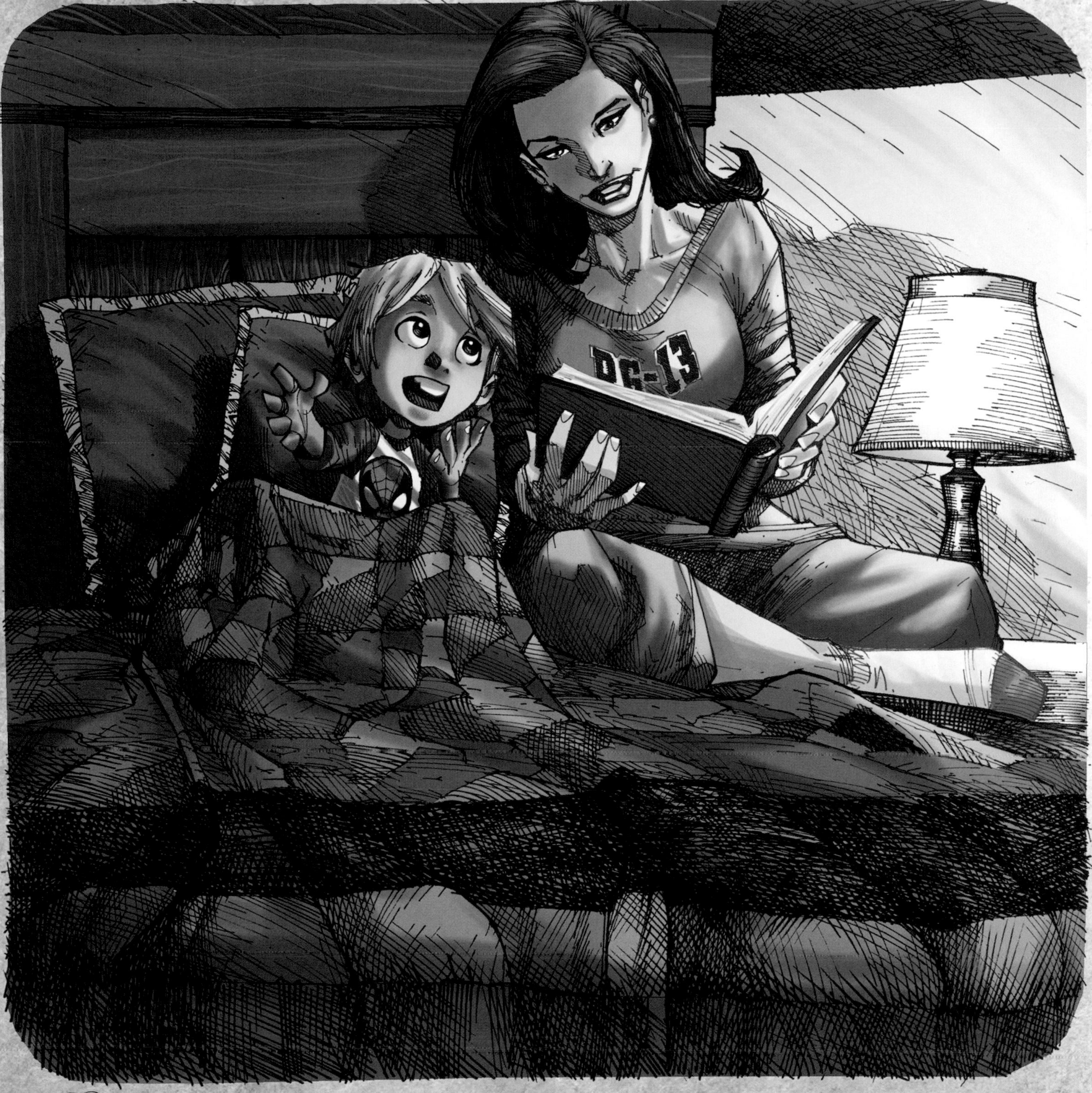
PG-13

Far across an unknown ocean, a million miles from where you are now is a land of make-believe. ARE YOU CLOSING YOUR EYES?

Then imagine you're turning in circles. And if you go towards the fingernail moon until it falls behind the hills you'll come upon an enchanted forest known as FABLEWOOD, where all of the stories that have ever been told live together.

A sto-wy! I wanna sto-wy!

WHICH STORY WOULD YOU LIKE TO HEAR?

Widin' Hood!

VERY WELL. ARE YOU RESTING COMFORTABLY?

Uh-huh.

THEN I'LL BEGIN. This is the story of LITTLE RED RIDING HOOD AND THE BIG, BAD WOLF...

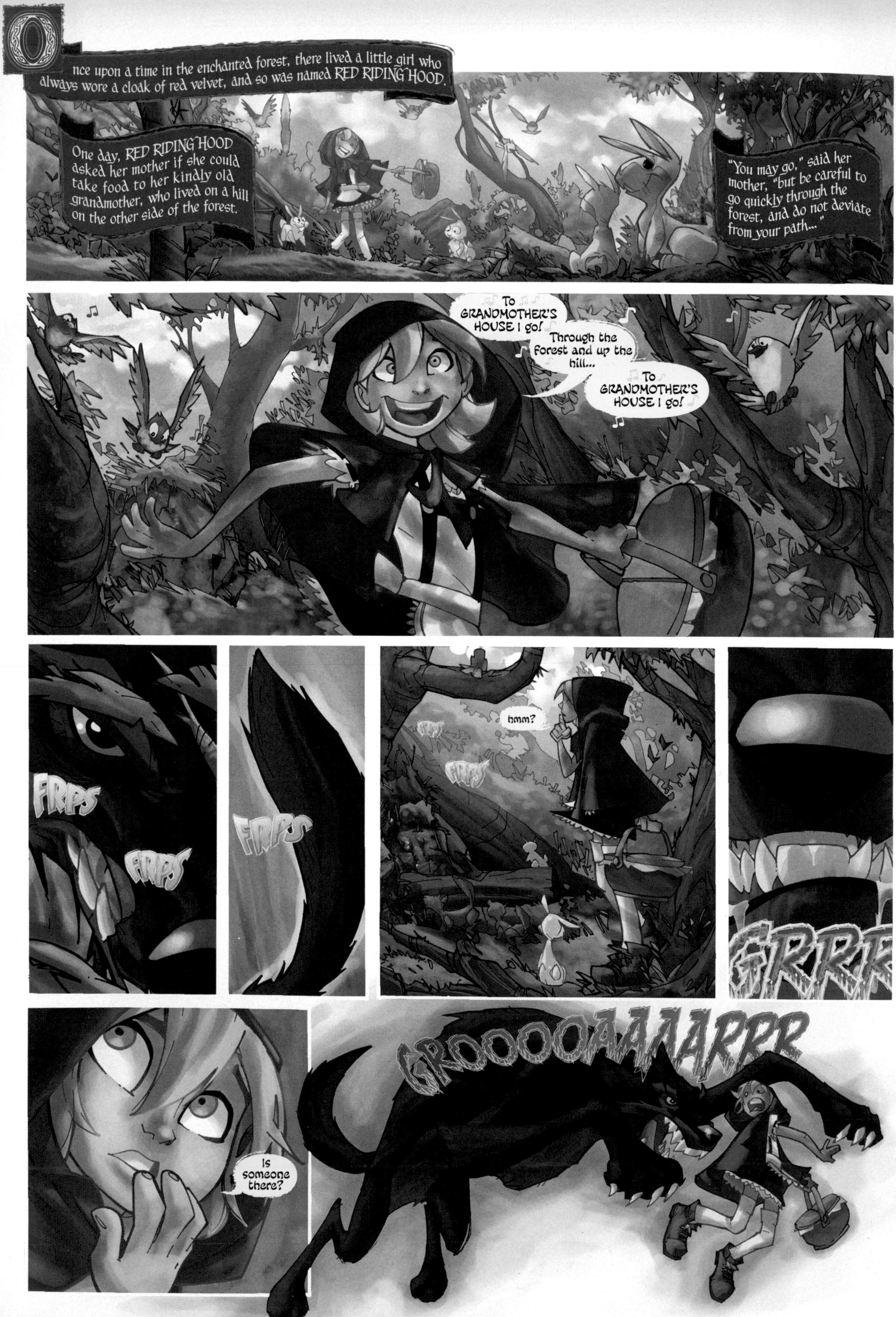
Once upon a time in the enchanted forest, there lived a little girl who always wore a cloak of red velvet, and so was named RED RIDING HOOD.
One day, RED RIDING HOOD asked her mother if she could take food to her kindly old grandmother, who lived on a hill on the other side of the forest.
"You may go," said her mother, "but be careful to go quickly through the forest, and do not deviate from your path..."
To GRANDMOTHER'S HOUSE I go!
Through the forest and up the hill...
To GRANDMOTHER'S HOUSE I go!
FRPS
FRPS
FRPS
hmm?
FRPS
FRPS
GRRR
Is someone there?
GROOOOAAAARRR

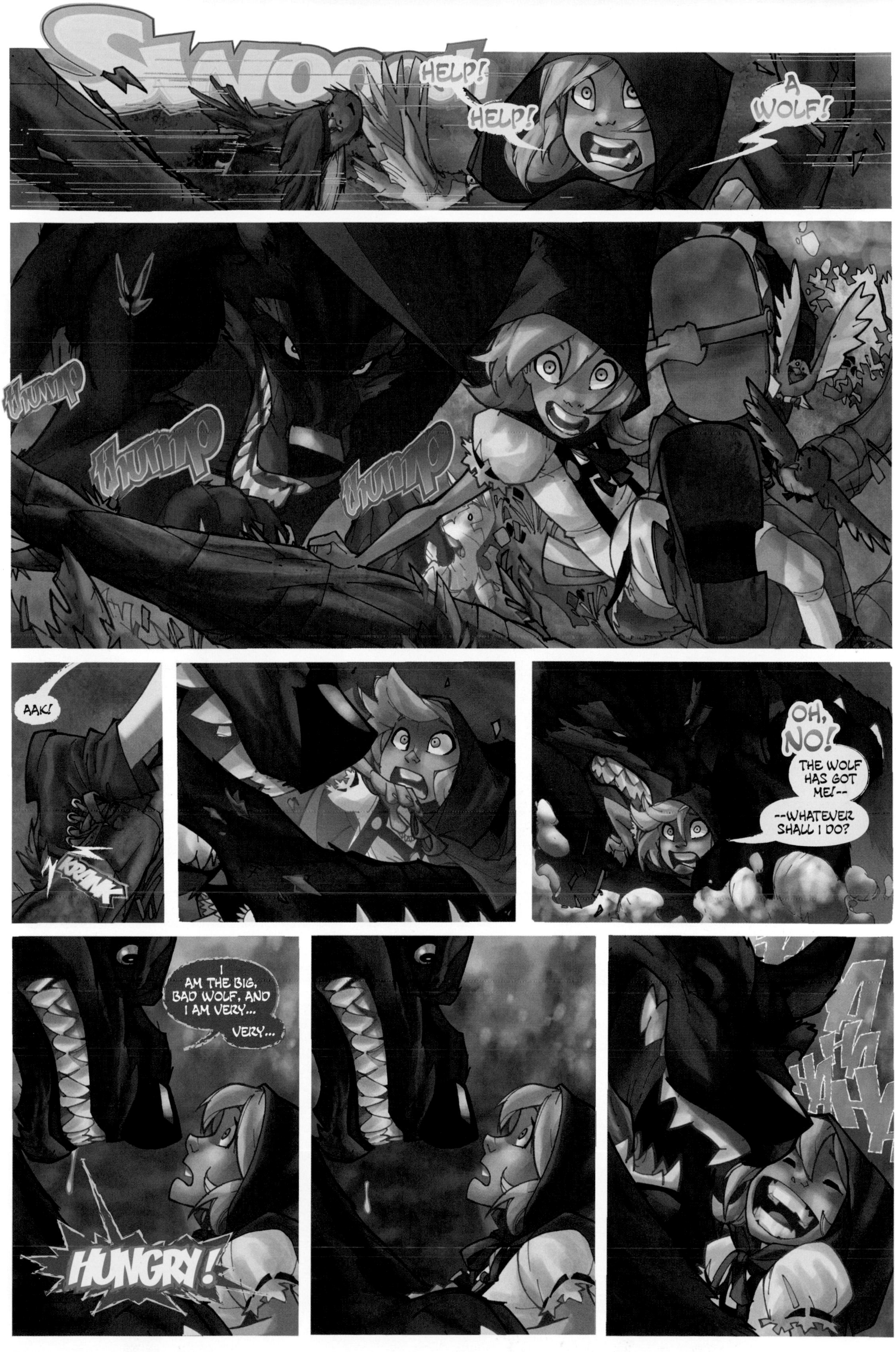
HELP!
HELP!
A WOLF!
thump
thump
thump
AAK!
KRANK
OH, NO!
THE WOLF HAS GOT ME!--
--WHATEVER SHALL I DO?
I AM THE BIG, BAD WOLF, AND I AM VERY...
VERY...
HUNGRY!

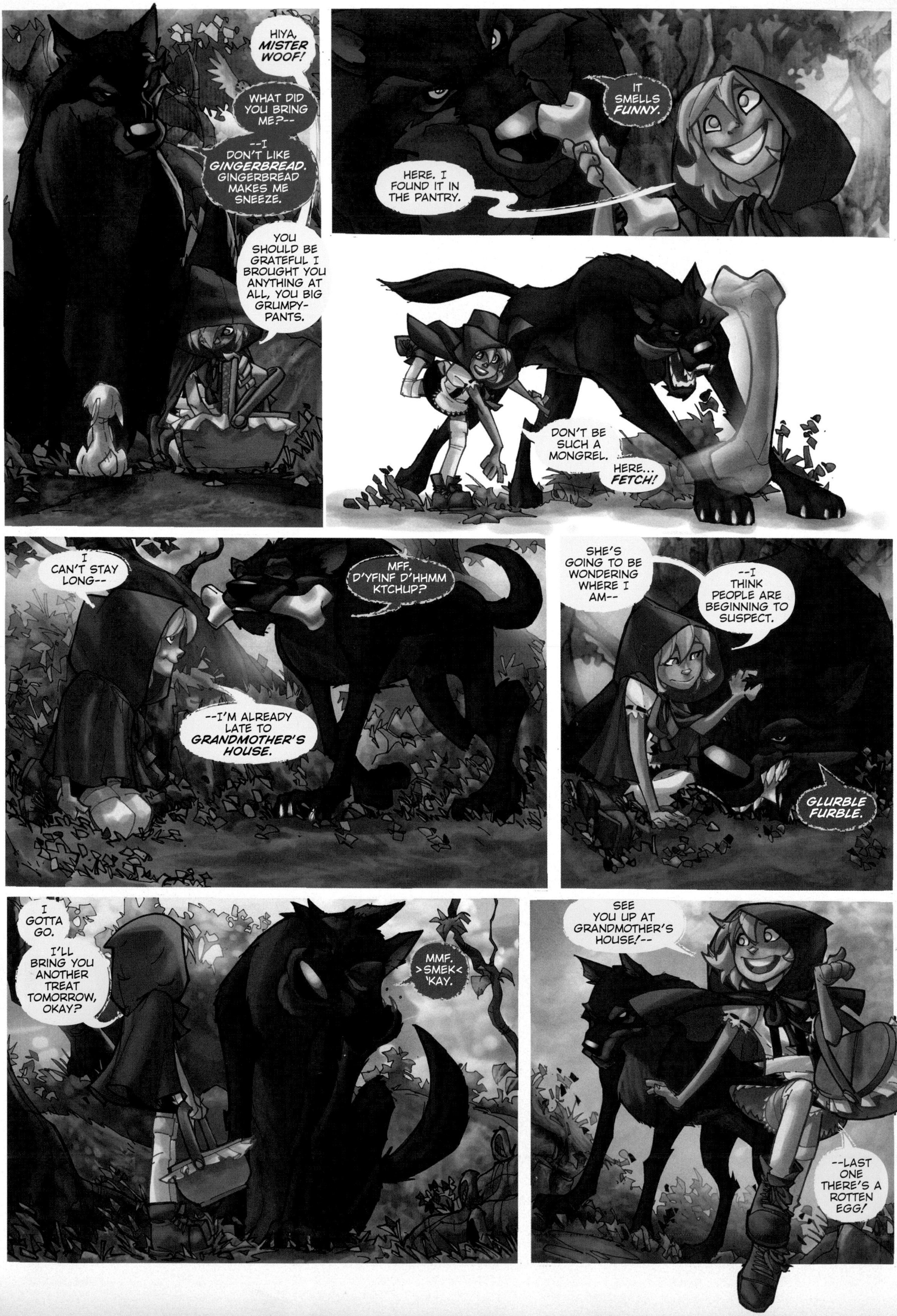
HIYA, MISTER WOOF!
WHAT DID YOU BRING ME?--
--I DON'T LIKE GINGERBREAD. GINGERBREAD MAKES ME SNEEZE.
YOU SHOULD BE GRATEFUL I BROUGHT YOU ANYTHING AT ALL, YOU BIG GRUMPY-PANTS.
IT SMELLS FUNNY.
HERE. I FOUND IT IN THE PANTRY.
DON'T BE SUCH A MONGREL.
HERE... FETCH!
I CAN'T STAY LONG--
MFF. D'YFINF D'HHMM KTCHUP?
--I'M ALREADY LATE TO GRANDMOTHER'S HOUSE.
SHE'S GOING TO BE WONDERING WHERE I AM--
--I THINK PEOPLE ARE BEGINNING TO SUSPECT.
GLURBLE FURBLE.
I GOTTA GO.
I'LL BRING YOU ANOTHER TREAT TOMORROW, OKAY?
MMF. >SMEK< 'KAY.
SEE YOU UP AT GRANDMOTHER'S HOUSE!--
--LAST ONE THERE'S A ROTTEN EGG!

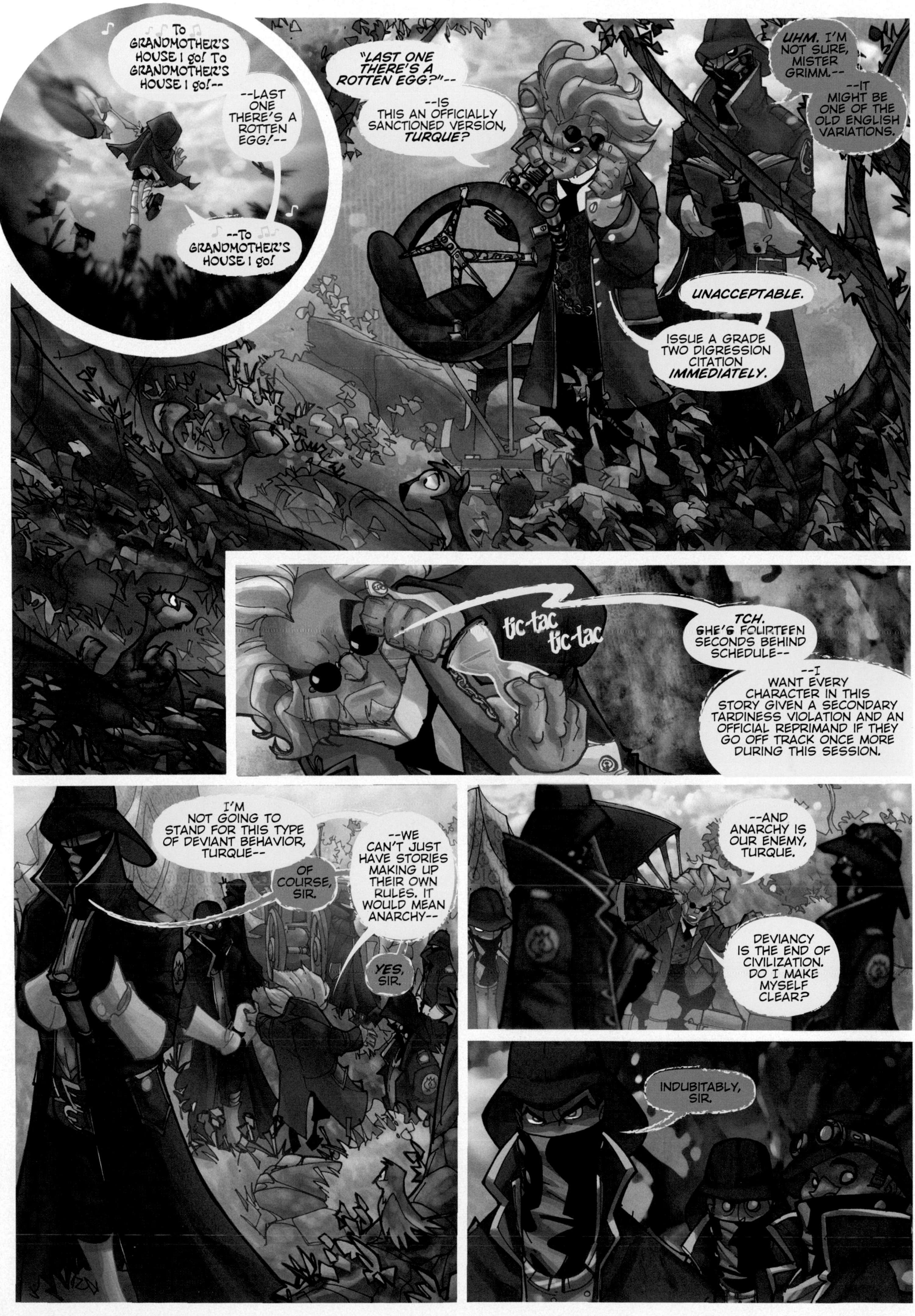
To GRANDMOTHER'S HOUSE I go! To GRANDMOTHER'S HOUSE I go!--
--LAST ONE THERE'S A ROTTEN EGG!--
--To GRANDMOTHER'S HOUSE I go!
"LAST ONE THERE'S A ROTTEN EGG?"--
--IS THIS AN OFFICIALLY SANCTIONED VERSION, TURQUE?
UHM. I'M NOT SURE, MISTER GRIMM.--
--IT MIGHT BE ONE OF THE OLD ENGLISH VARIATIONS.
UNACCEPTABLE.
ISSUE A GRADE TWO DIGRESSION CITATION IMMEDIATELY.
tic-tac tic-tac
TCH. SHE'S FOURTEEN SECONDS BEHIND SCHEDULE--
--I WANT EVERY CHARACTER IN THIS STORY GIVEN A SECONDARY TARDINESS VIOLATION AND AN OFFICIAL REPRIMAND IF THEY GO OFF TRACK ONCE MORE DURING THIS SESSION.
I'M NOT GOING TO STAND FOR THIS TYPE OF DEVIANT BEHAVIOR, TURQUE--
OF COURSE, SIR.
--WE CAN'T JUST HAVE STORIES MAKING UP THEIR OWN RULES. IT WOULD MEAN ANARCHY--
YES, SIR.
--AND ANARCHY IS OUR ENEMY, TURQUE.
DEVIANCY IS THE END OF CIVILIZATION. DO I MAKE MYSELF CLEAR?
INDUBITABLY, SIR.

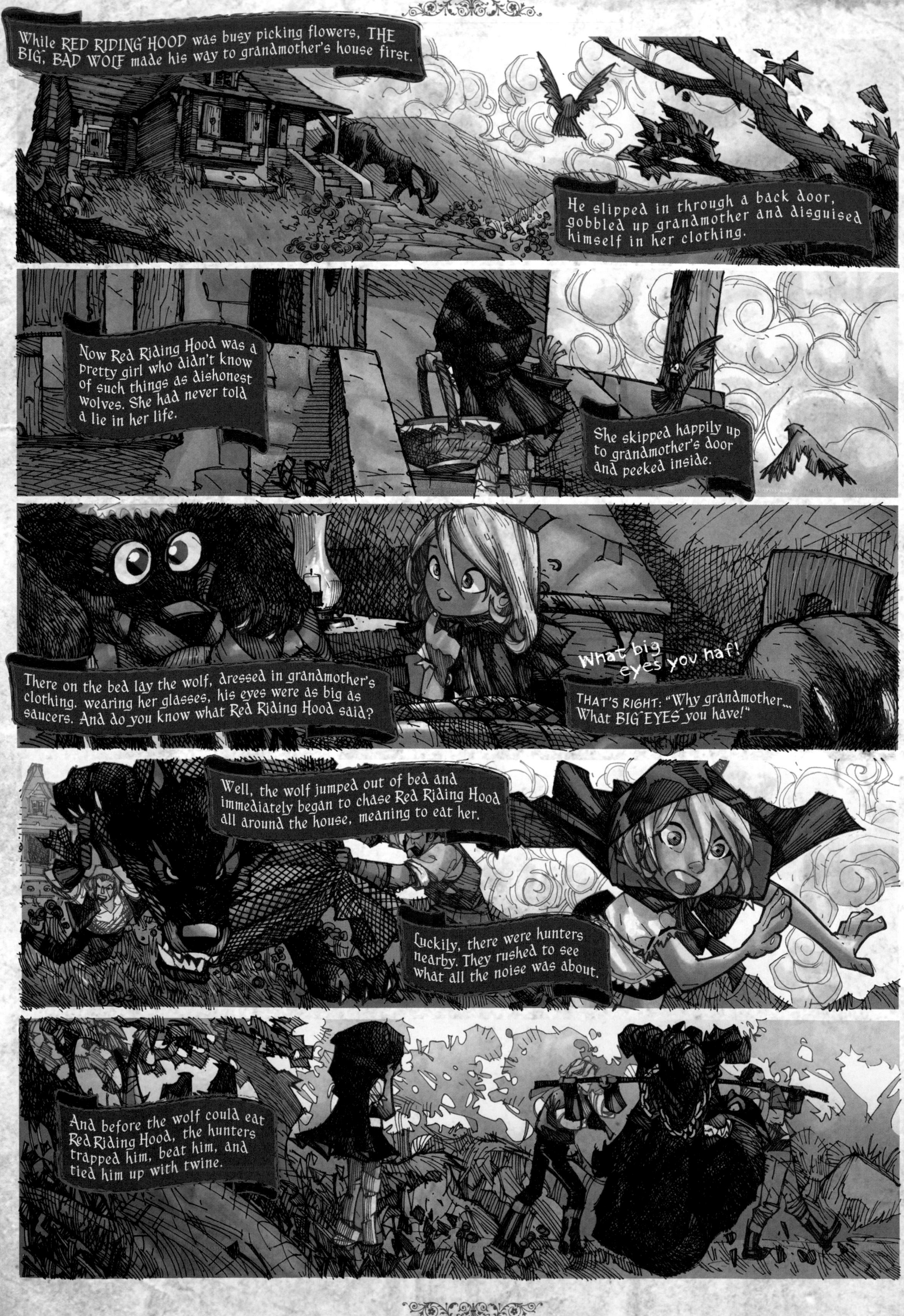

While RED RIDING HOOD was busy picking flowers, THE BIG, BAD WOLF made his way to grandmother's house first.
He slipped in through a back door, gobbled up grandmother and disguised himself in her clothing.
Now Red Riding Hood was a pretty girl who didn't know of such things as dishonest wolves. She had never told a lie in her life.
She skipped happily up to grandmother's door and peeked inside.
There on the bed lay the wolf, dressed in grandmother's clothing. wearing her glasses, his eyes were as big as saucers. And do you know what Red Riding Hood said?
What big eyes you haf!
THAT'S RIGHT: "Why grandmother... What BIG EYES you have!"
Well, the wolf jumped out of bed and immediately began to chase Red Riding Hood all around the house, meaning to eat her.
Luckily, there were hunters nearby. They rushed to see what all the noise was about.
And before the wolf could eat Red Riding Hood, the hunters trapped him, beat him, and tied him up with twine.

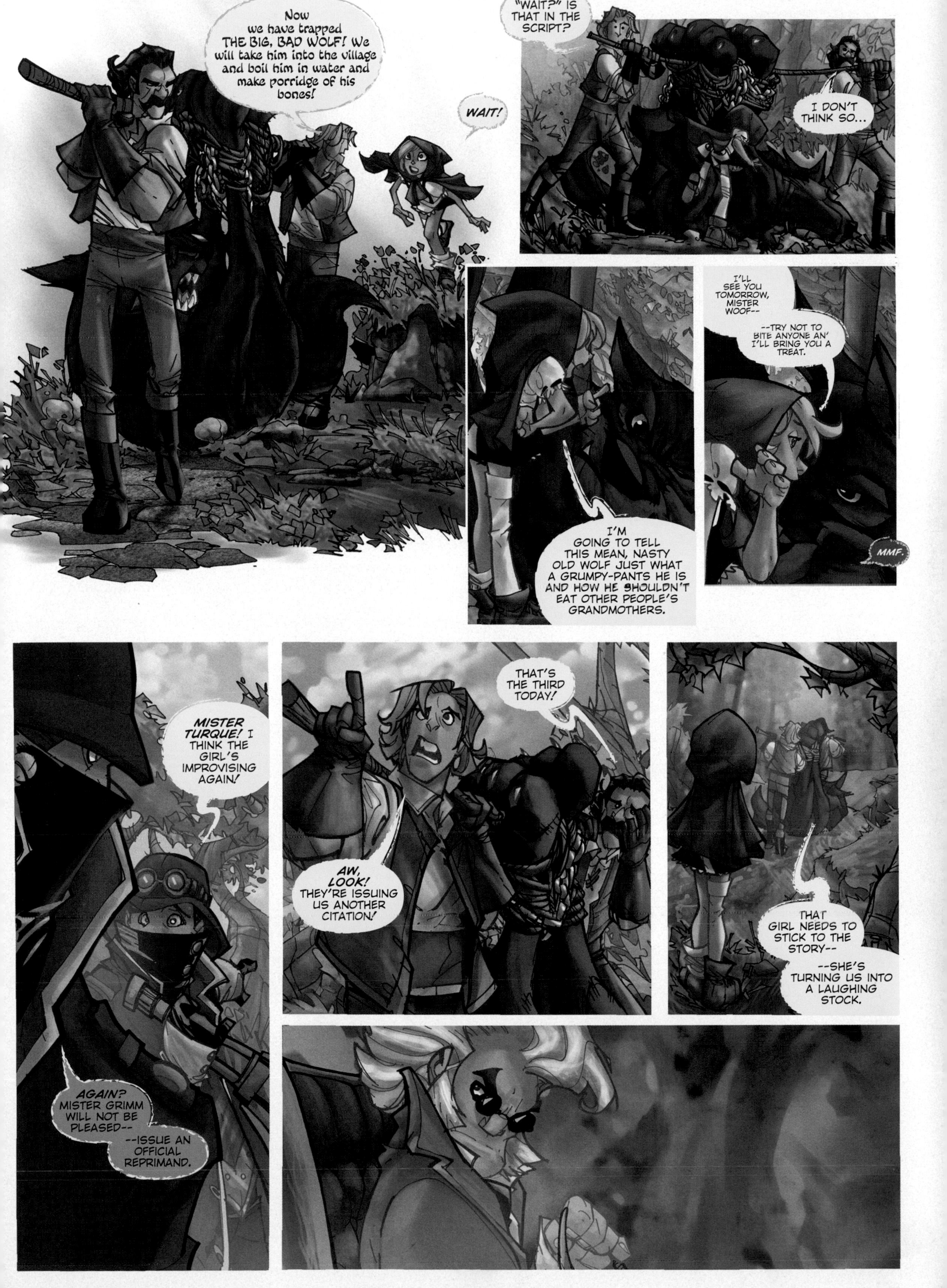

Now we have trapped THE BIG, BAD WOLF! We will take him into the village and boil him in water and make porridge of his bones!
WAIT!
"WAIT?" IS THAT IN THE SCRIPT?
I DON'T THINK SO...
I'M GOING TO TELL THIS MEAN, NASTY OLD WOLF JUST WHAT A GRUMPY-PANTS HE IS AND HOW HE SHOULDN'T EAT OTHER PEOPLE'S GRANDMOTHERS.
I'LL SEE YOU TOMORROW, MISTER WOOF--
--TRY NOT TO BITE ANYONE AN' I'LL BRING YOU A TREAT.
MMF.
MISTER TURQUE! I THINK THE GIRL'S IMPROVISING AGAIN!
AGAIN? MISTER GRIMM WILL NOT BE PLEASED--
--ISSUE AN OFFICIAL REPRIMAND.
THAT'S THE THIRD TODAY!
AW, LOOK! THEY'RE ISSUING US ANOTHER CITATION!
THAT GIRL NEEDS TO STICK TO THE STORY--
--SHE'S TURNING US INTO A LAUGHING STOCK.

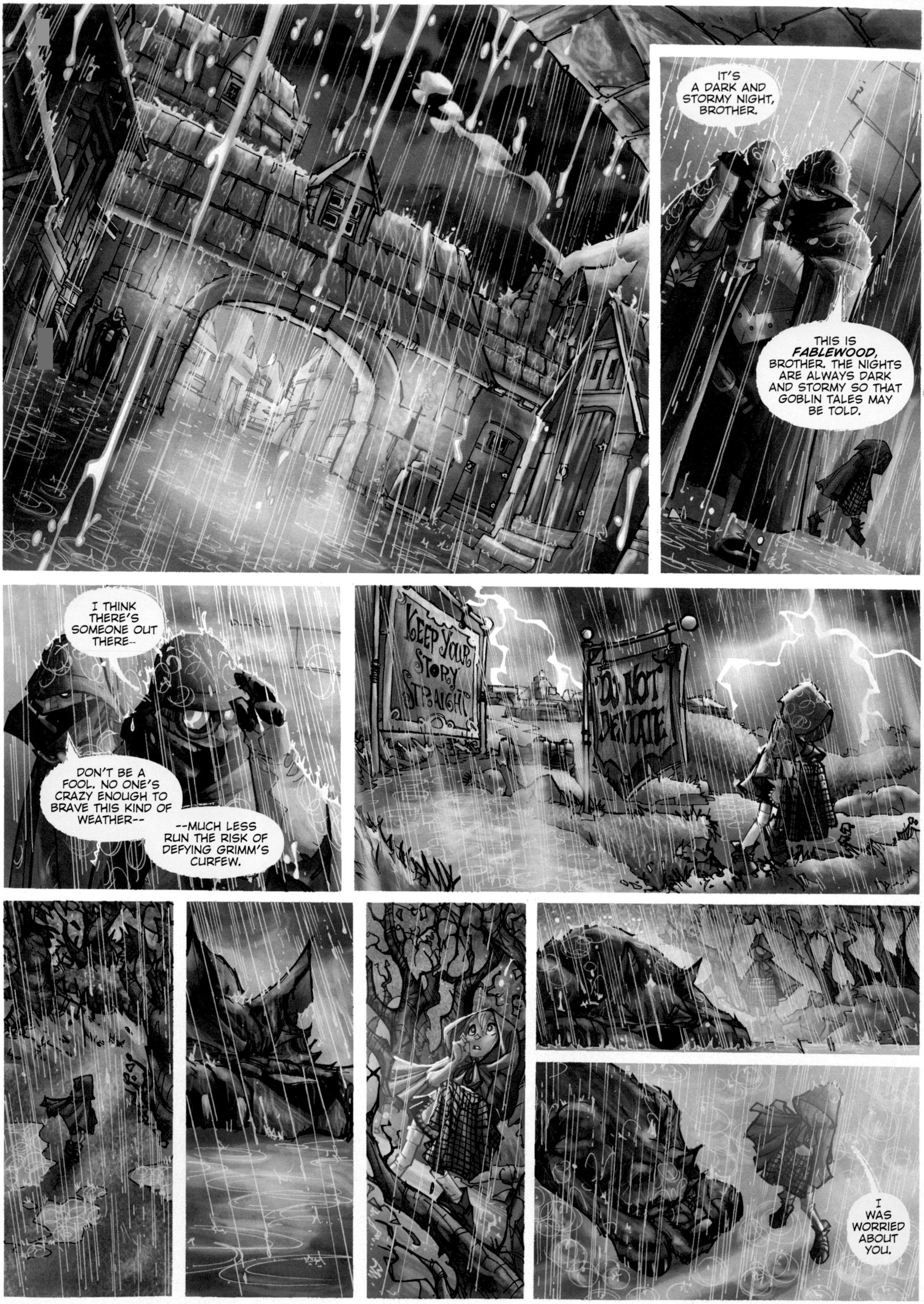
IT'S A DARK AND STORMY NIGHT, BROTHER.
THIS IS FABLEWOOD, BROTHER. THE NIGHTS ARE ALWAYS DARK AND STORMY SO THAT GOBLIN TALES MAY BE TOLD.
I THINK THERE'S SOMEONE OUT THERE--
DON'T BE A FOOL. NO ONE'S CRAZY ENOUGH TO BRAVE THIS KIND OF WEATHER--
--MUCH LESS RUN THE RISK OF DEFYING GRIMM'S CURFEW.
KEEP YOUR STORY STRAIGHT
DO NOT DEVIATE
I WAS WORRIED ABOUT YOU.

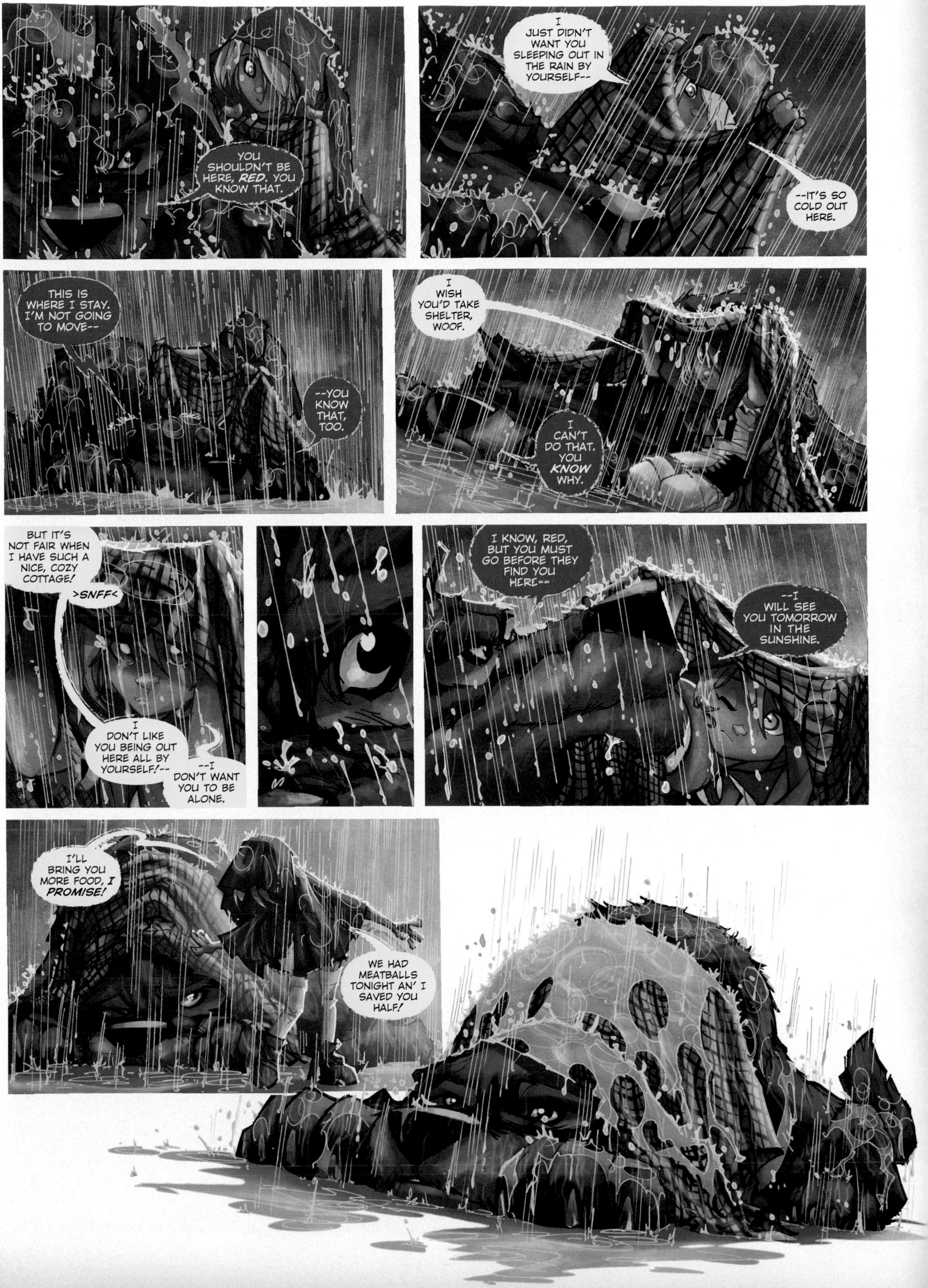
YOU SHOULDN'T BE HERE, ***RED***. YOU KNOW THAT.
I JUST DIDN'T WANT YOU SLEEPING OUT IN THE RAIN BY YOURSELF--
--IT'S SO COLD OUT HERE.
THIS IS WHERE I STAY. I'M NOT GOING TO MOVE--
--YOU KNOW THAT, TOO.
I WISH YOU'D TAKE SHELTER, WOOF.
I CAN'T DO THAT. YOU ***KNOW*** WHY.
BUT IT'S NOT FAIR WHEN I HAVE SUCH A NICE, COZY COTTAGE*!*
>***SNFF***<
I DON'T LIKE YOU BEING OUT HERE ALL BY YOURSELF*!*--
--I DON'T WANT YOU TO BE ALONE.
I KNOW, RED, BUT YOU MUST GO BEFORE THEY FIND YOU HERE--
--I WILL SEE YOU TOMORROW IN THE SUNSHINE.
I'LL BRING YOU MORE FOOD, ***I PROMISE!***
WE HAD MEATBALLS TONIGHT AN' I SAVED YOU HALF*!*

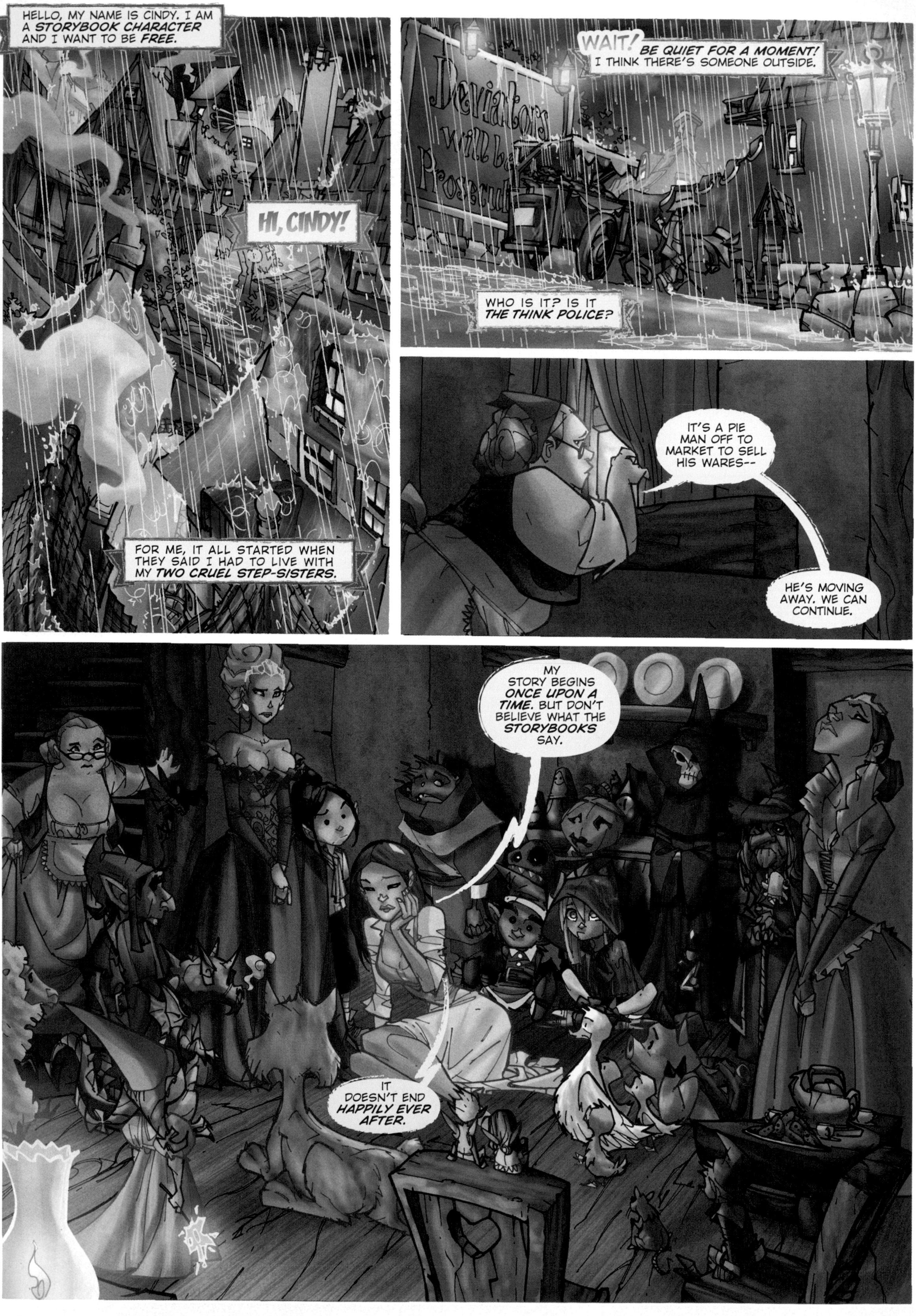
HELLO, MY NAME IS CINDY. I AM A STORYBOOK CHARACTER AND I WANT TO BE FREE.
HI, CINDY!
FOR ME, IT ALL STARTED WHEN THEY SAID I HAD TO LIVE WITH MY TWO CRUEL STEP-SISTERS.
WAIT! BE QUIET FOR A MOMENT! I THINK THERE'S SOMEONE OUTSIDE.
Deviators Will be Prosecut
WHO IS IT? IS IT THE THINK POLICE?
IT'S A PIE MAN OFF TO MARKET TO SELL HIS WARES--
HE'S MOVING AWAY. WE CAN CONTINUE.
MY STORY BEGINS ONCE UPON A TIME. BUT DON'T BELIEVE WHAT THE STORYBOOKS SAY.
IT DOESN'T END HAPPILY EVER AFTER.

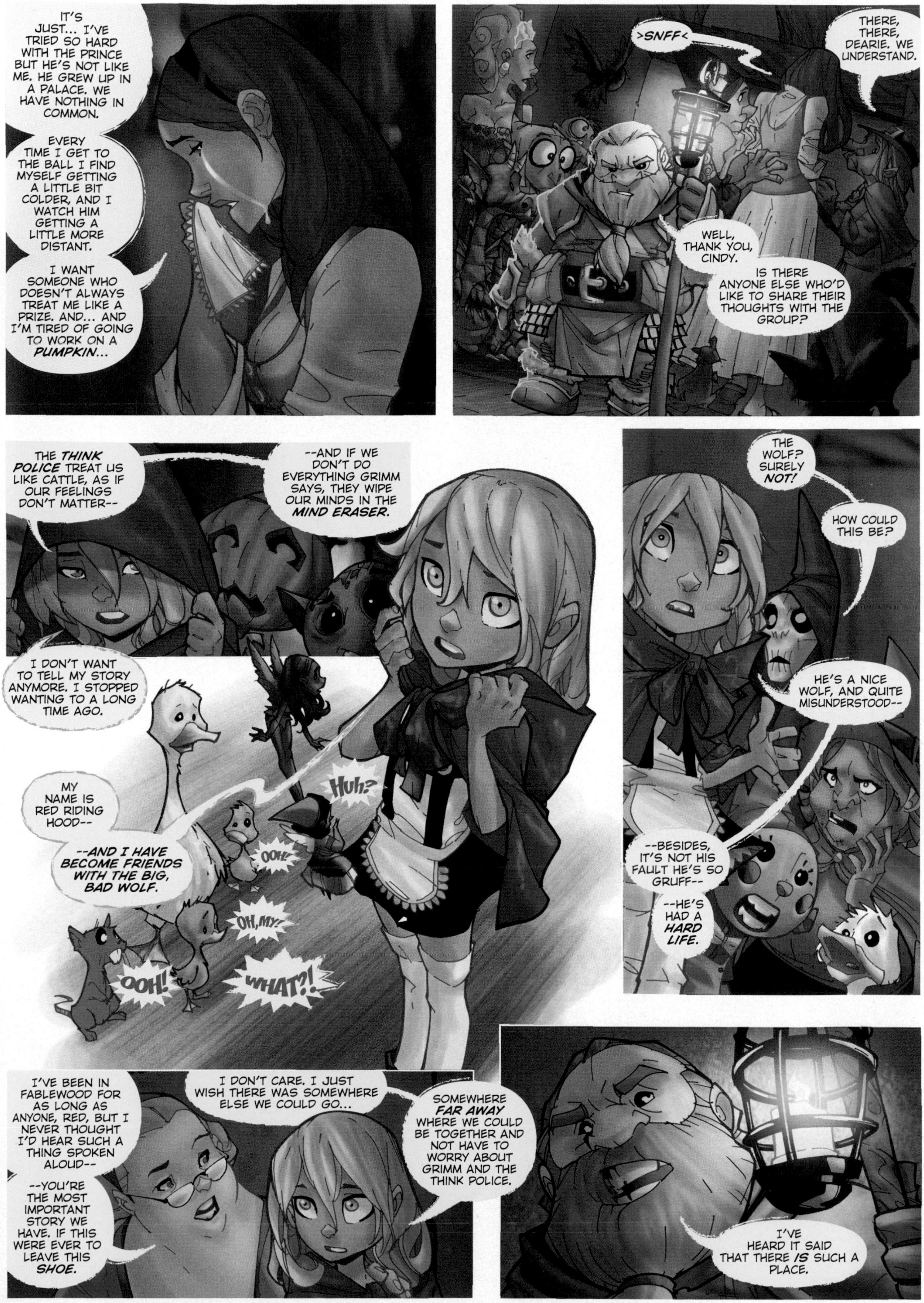
IT'S JUST... I'VE TRIED SO HARD WITH THE PRINCE BUT HE'S NOT LIKE ME. HE GREW UP IN A PALACE. WE HAVE NOTHING IN COMMON.
EVERY TIME I GET TO THE BALL I FIND MYSELF GETTING A LITTLE BIT COLDER, AND I WATCH HIM GETTING A LITTLE MORE DISTANT.
I WANT SOMEONE WHO DOESN'T ALWAYS TREAT ME LIKE A PRIZE. AND... AND I'M TIRED OF GOING TO WORK ON A *PUMPKIN*...
>SNFF<
THERE, THERE, DEARIE. WE UNDERSTAND.
WELL, THANK YOU, CINDY.
IS THERE ANYONE ELSE WHO'D LIKE TO SHARE THEIR THOUGHTS WITH THE GROUP?
THE *THINK POLICE* TREAT US LIKE CATTLE, AS IF OUR FEELINGS DON'T MATTER--
--AND IF WE DON'T DO EVERYTHING GRIMM SAYS, THEY WIPE OUR MINDS IN THE *MIND ERASER.*
I DON'T WANT TO TELL MY STORY ANYMORE. I STOPPED WANTING TO A LONG TIME AGO.
MY NAME IS RED RIDING HOOD--
--AND I HAVE BECOME FRIENDS WITH THE BIG, BAD WOLF.
HUH?
OOH!
OH, MY!
OOH!
WHAT?!
THE WOLF? SURELY *NOT!*
HOW COULD THIS BE?
HE'S A NICE WOLF, AND QUITE MISUNDERSTOOD--
--BESIDES, IT'S NOT HIS FAULT HE'S SO GRUFF--
--HE'S HAD A *HARD LIFE.*
I'VE BEEN IN FABLEWOOD FOR AS LONG AS ANYONE, RED, BUT I NEVER THOUGHT I'D HEAR SUCH A THING SPOKEN ALOUD--
--YOU'RE THE MOST IMPORTANT STORY WE HAVE. IF THIS WERE EVER TO LEAVE THIS *SHOE.*
I DON'T CARE. I JUST WISH THERE WAS SOMEWHERE ELSE WE COULD GO...
SOMEWHERE *FAR AWAY* WHERE WE COULD BE TOGETHER AND NOT HAVE TO WORRY ABOUT GRIMM AND THE THINK POLICE.
I'VE HEARD IT SAID THAT THERE *IS* SUCH A PLACE.

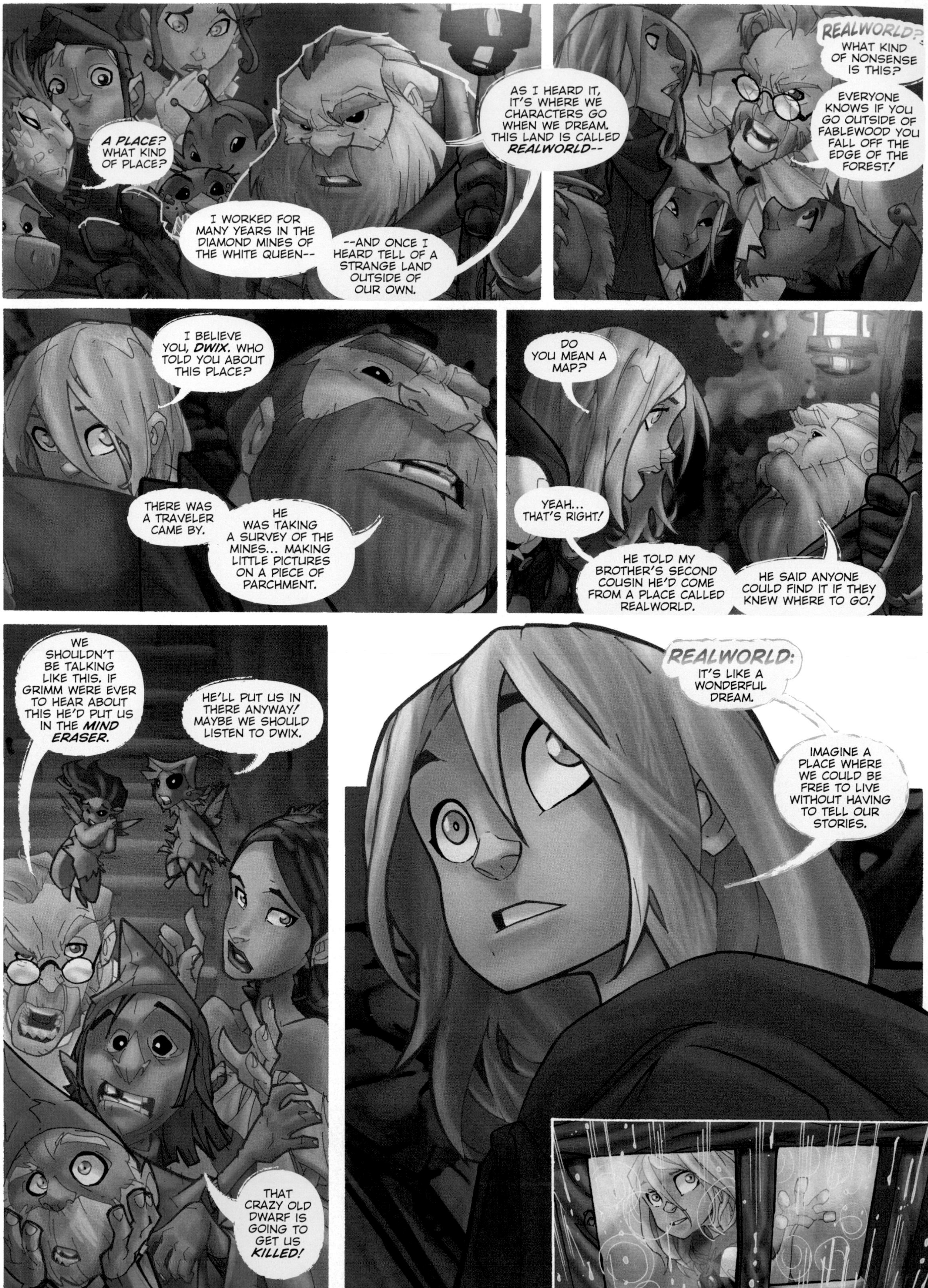

A PLACE? WHAT KIND OF PLACE?
AS I HEARD IT, IT'S WHERE WE CHARACTERS GO WHEN WE DREAM. THIS LAND IS CALLED REALWORLD--
I WORKED FOR MANY YEARS IN THE DIAMOND MINES OF THE WHITE QUEEN--
--AND ONCE I HEARD TELL OF A STRANGE LAND OUTSIDE OF OUR OWN.
REALWORLD? WHAT KIND OF NONSENSE IS THIS?
EVERYONE KNOWS IF YOU GO OUTSIDE OF FABLEWOOD YOU FALL OFF THE EDGE OF THE FOREST!
I BELIEVE YOU, DWIX. WHO TOLD YOU ABOUT THIS PLACE?
THERE WAS A TRAVELER CAME BY.
HE WAS TAKING A SURVEY OF THE MINES... MAKING LITTLE PICTURES ON A PIECE OF PARCHMENT.
DO YOU MEAN A MAP?
YEAH... THAT'S RIGHT!
HE TOLD MY BROTHER'S SECOND COUSIN HE'D COME FROM A PLACE CALLED REALWORLD.
HE SAID ANYONE COULD FIND IT IF THEY KNEW WHERE TO GO!
WE SHOULDN'T BE TALKING LIKE THIS. IF GRIMM WERE EVER TO HEAR ABOUT THIS HE'D PUT US IN THE MIND ERASER.
HE'LL PUT US IN THERE ANYWAY! MAYBE WE SHOULD LISTEN TO DWIX.
THAT CRAZY OLD DWARF IS GOING TO GET US KILLED!
REALWORLD: IT'S LIKE A WONDERFUL DREAM.
IMAGINE A PLACE WHERE WE COULD BE FREE TO LIVE WITHOUT HAVING TO TELL OUR STORIES.

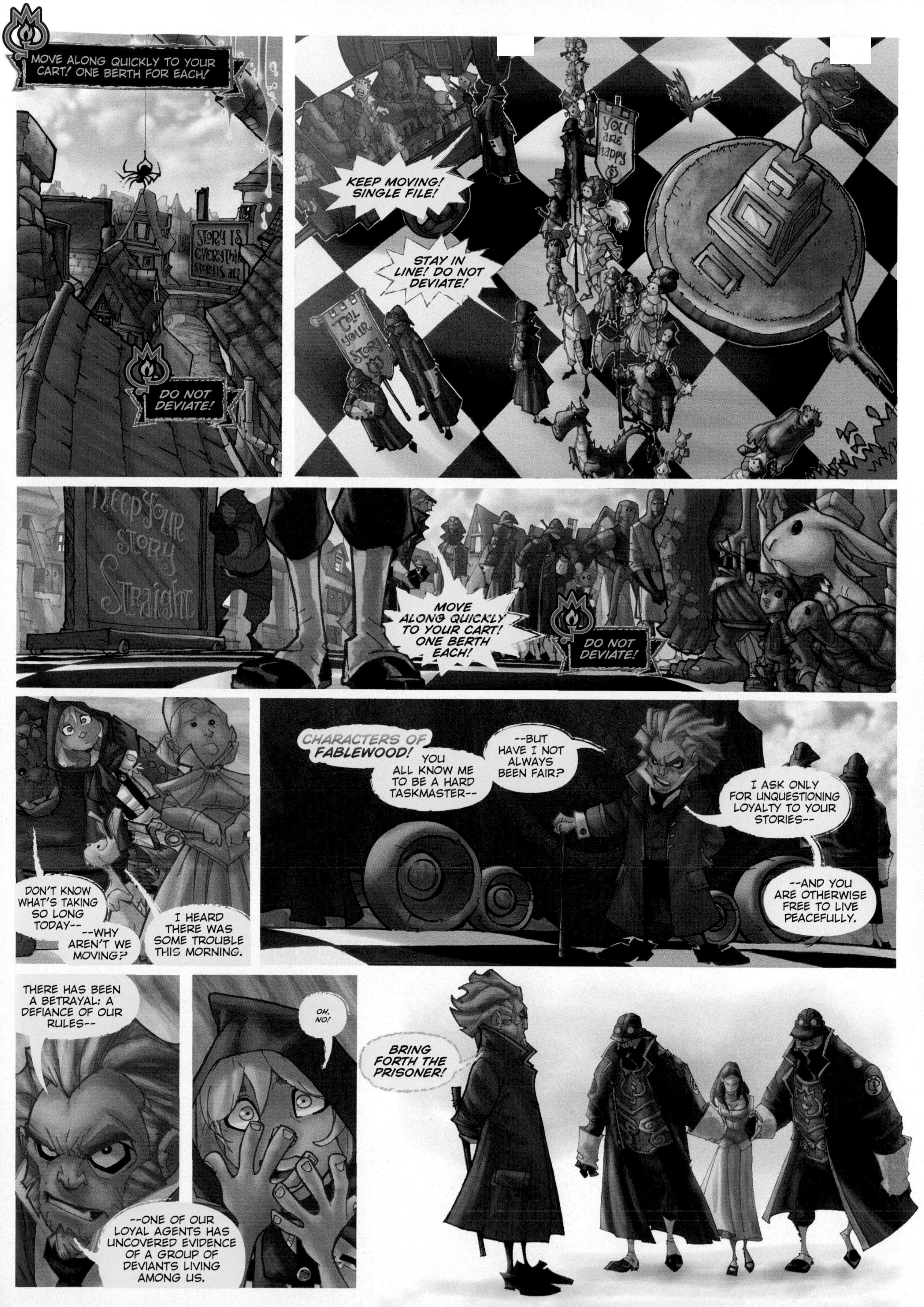

MOVE ALONG QUICKLY TO YOUR CART! ONE BERTH FOR EACH!
STORY IS EVERYTHIN STORY IS ALL
DO NOT DEVIATE!
KEEP MOVING! SINGLE FILE!
YOU ARE HAPPY
STAY IN LINE! DO NOT DEVIATE!
TELL YOUR STORY
KEEP YOUR STORY STRAIGHT
MOVE ALONG QUICKLY TO YOUR CART! ONE BERTH EACH!
DO NOT DEVIATE!
DON'T KNOW WHAT'S TAKING SO LONG TODAY--
--WHY AREN'T WE MOVING?
I HEARD THERE WAS SOME TROUBLE THIS MORNING.
CHARACTERS OF FABLEWOOD!
YOU ALL KNOW ME TO BE A HARD TASKMASTER--
--BUT HAVE I NOT ALWAYS BEEN FAIR?
I ASK ONLY FOR UNQUESTIONING LOYALTY TO YOUR STORIES--
--AND YOU ARE OTHERWISE FREE TO LIVE PEACEFULLY.
THERE HAS BEEN A BETRAYAL: A DEFIANCE OF OUR RULES--
--ONE OF OUR LOYAL AGENTS HAS UNCOVERED EVIDENCE OF A GROUP OF DEVIANTS LIVING AMONG US.
OH, NO!
BRING FORTH THE PRISONER!

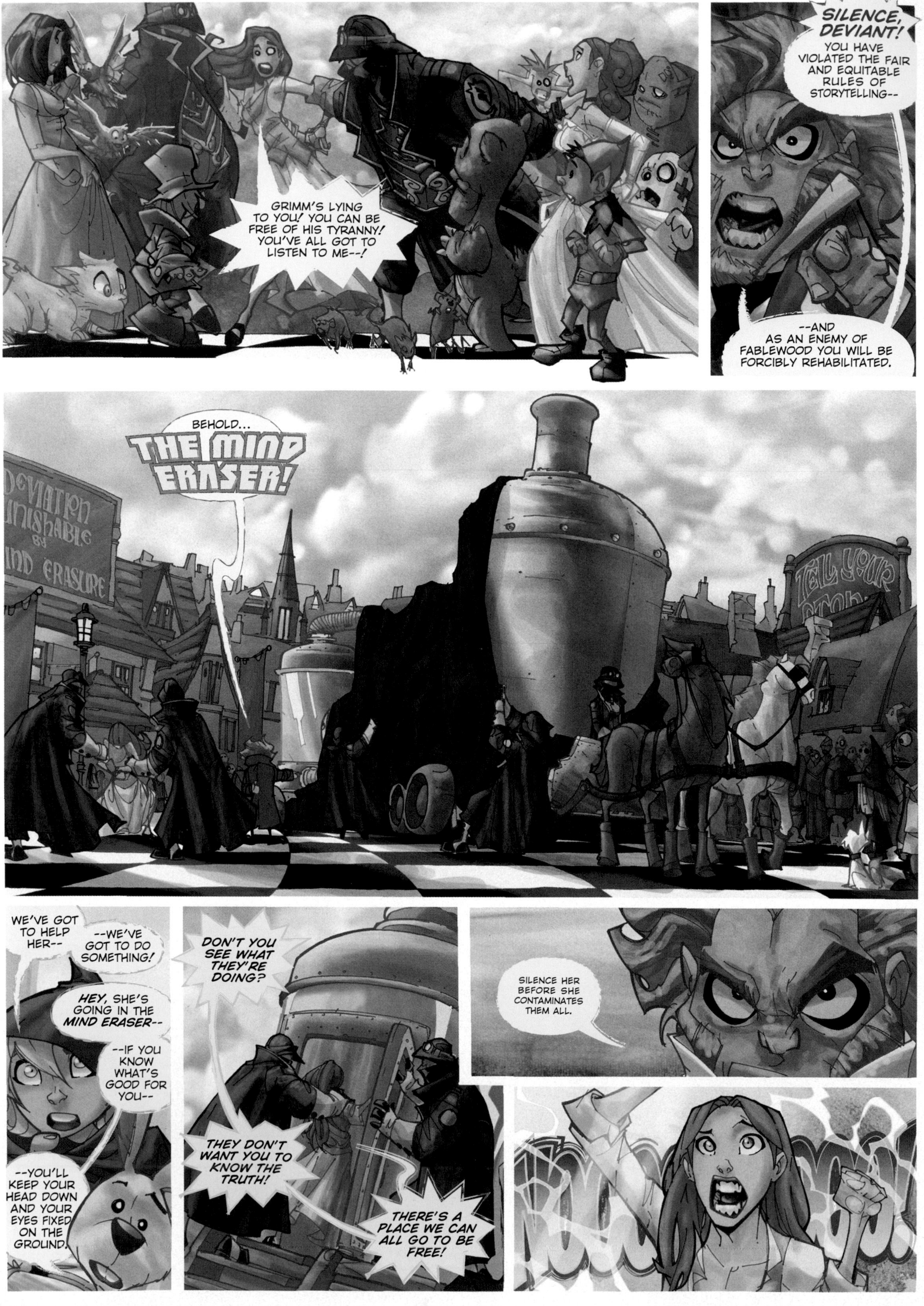
GRIMM'S LYING TO YOU! YOU CAN BE FREE OF HIS TYRANNY! YOU'VE ALL GOT TO LISTEN TO ME--!
SILENCE, DEVIANT!
YOU HAVE VIOLATED THE FAIR AND EQUITABLE RULES OF STORYTELLING--
--AND AS AN ENEMY OF FABLEWOOD YOU WILL BE FORCIBLY REHABILITATED.
BEHOLD...
THE MIND ERASER!
WE'VE GOT TO HELP HER--
--WE'VE GOT TO DO SOMETHING!
HEY, SHE'S GOING IN THE MIND ERASER--
--IF YOU KNOW WHAT'S GOOD FOR YOU--
--YOU'LL KEEP YOUR HEAD DOWN AND YOUR EYES FIXED ON THE GROUND.
DON'T YOU SEE WHAT THEY'RE DOING?
THEY DON'T WANT YOU TO KNOW THE TRUTH!
THERE'S A PLACE WE CAN ALL GO TO BE FREE!
SILENCE HER BEFORE SHE CONTAMINATES THEM ALL.

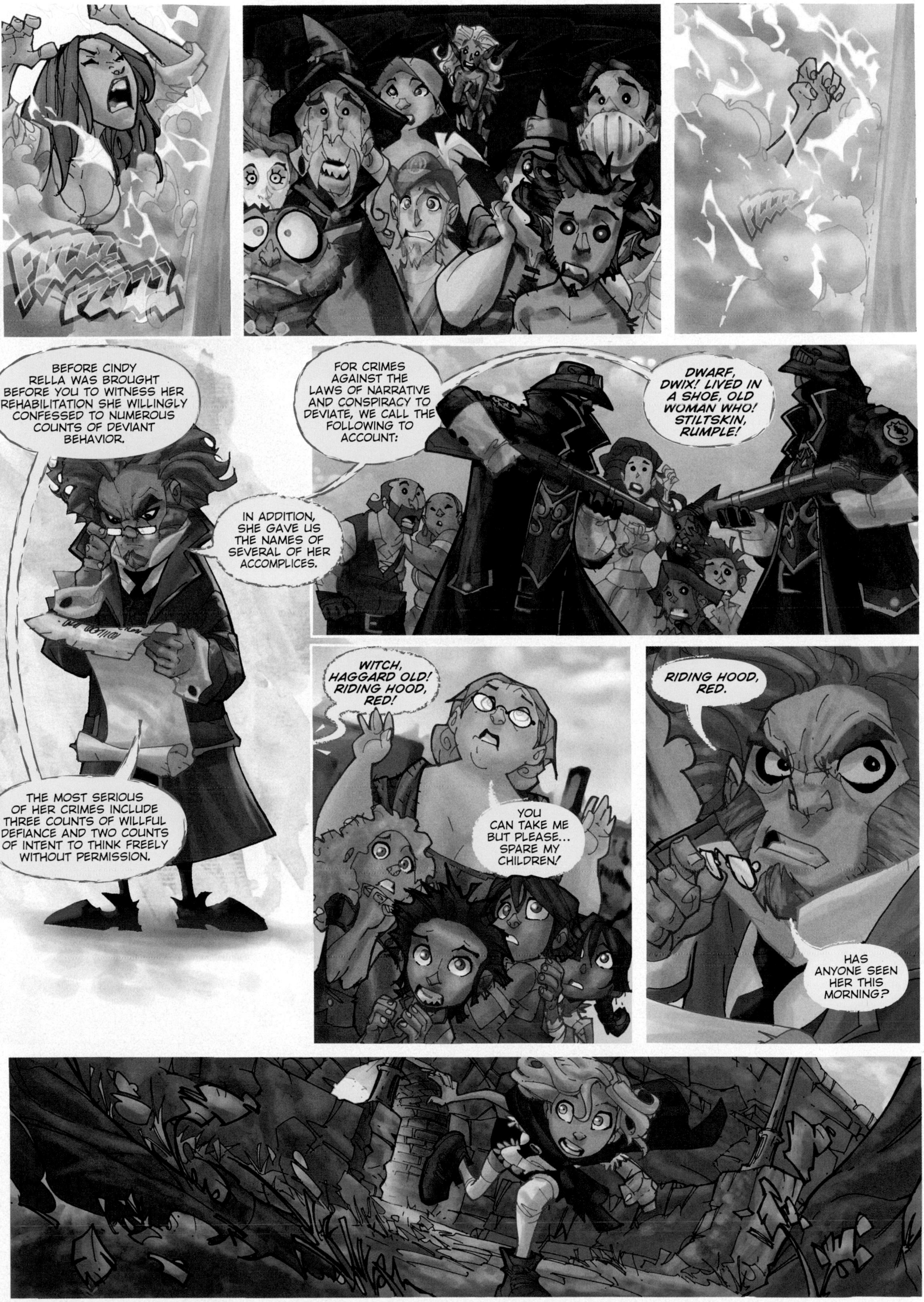
BEFORE CINDY RELLA WAS BROUGHT BEFORE YOU TO WITNESS HER REHABILITATION SHE WILLINGLY CONFESSED TO NUMEROUS COUNTS OF DEVIANT BEHAVIOR.
IN ADDITION, SHE GAVE US THE NAMES OF SEVERAL OF HER ACCOMPLICES.
THE MOST SERIOUS OF HER CRIMES INCLUDE THREE COUNTS OF WILLFUL DEFIANCE AND TWO COUNTS OF INTENT TO THINK FREELY WITHOUT PERMISSION.
FOR CRIMES AGAINST THE LAWS OF NARRATIVE AND CONSPIRACY TO DEVIATE, WE CALL THE FOLLOWING TO ACCOUNT:
DWARF, DWIX! LIVED IN A SHOE, OLD WOMAN WHO! STILTSKIN, RUMPLE!
WITCH, HAGGARD OLD! RIDING HOOD, RED!
YOU CAN TAKE ME BUT PLEASE... SPARE MY CHILDREN!
RIDING HOOD, RED.
HAS ANYONE SEEN HER THIS MORNING?

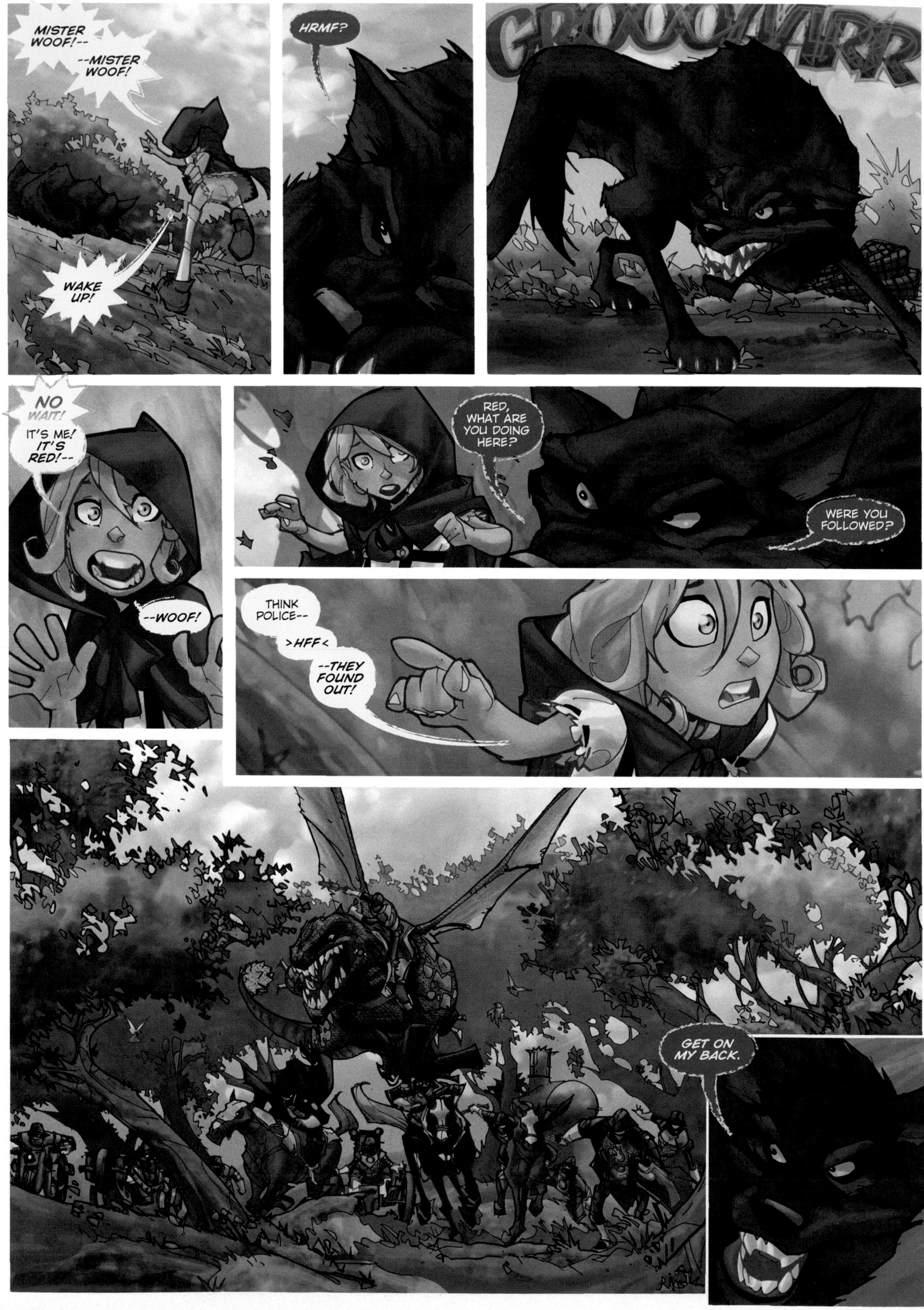
MISTER WOOF!--
--MISTER WOOF!
WAKE UP!
HRMF?
GROOOWRR
NO WAIT!
IT'S ME! IT'S RED!--
--WOOF!
RED, WHAT ARE YOU DOING HERE?
WERE YOU FOLLOWED?
THINK POLICE--
>HFF<
--THEY FOUND OUT!
GET ON MY BACK.

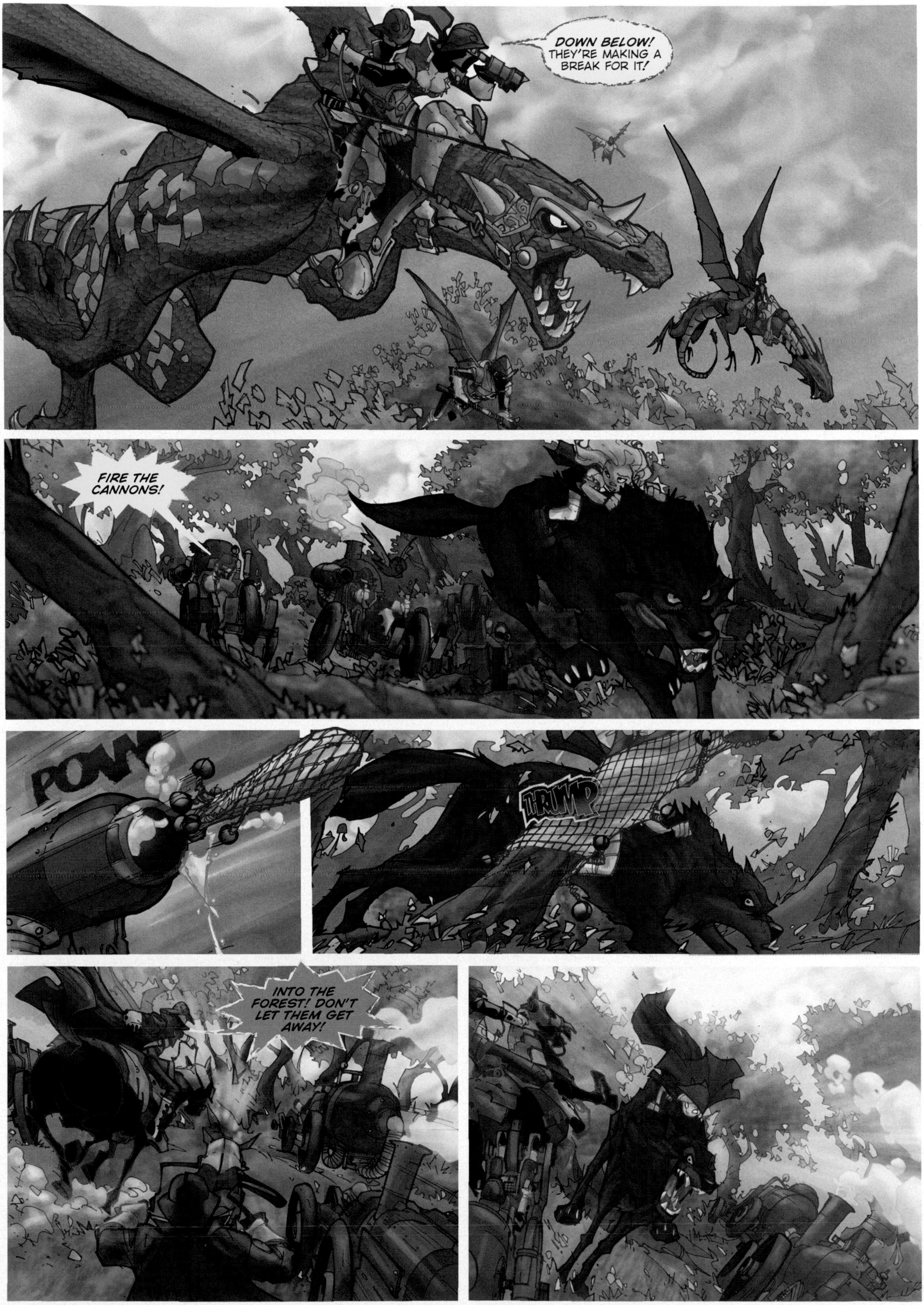
DOWN BELOW! THEY'RE MAKING A BREAK FOR IT!
FIRE THE CANNONS!
POW
THRUMP
INTO THE FOREST! DON'T LET THEM GET AWAY!

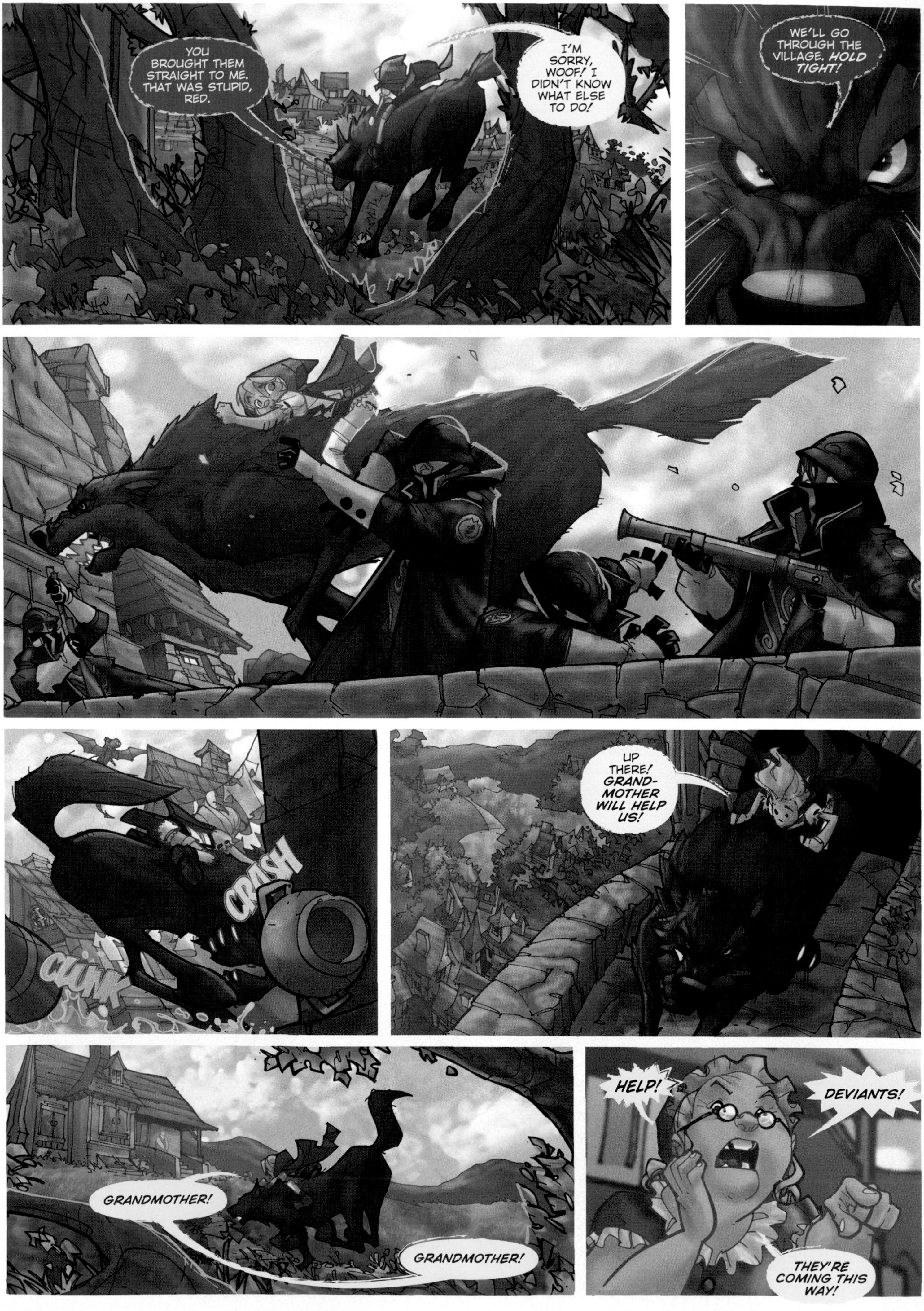
YOU BROUGHT THEM STRAIGHT TO ME. THAT WAS STUPID, RED.
I'M SORRY, WOOF! I DIDN'T KNOW WHAT ELSE TO DO!
WE'LL GO THROUGH THE VILLAGE. HOLD TIGHT!
CRASH
CLUNK
UP THERE! GRANDMOTHER WILL HELP US!
GRANDMOTHER!
GRANDMOTHER!
HELP!
DEVIANTS!
THEY'RE COMING THIS WAY!

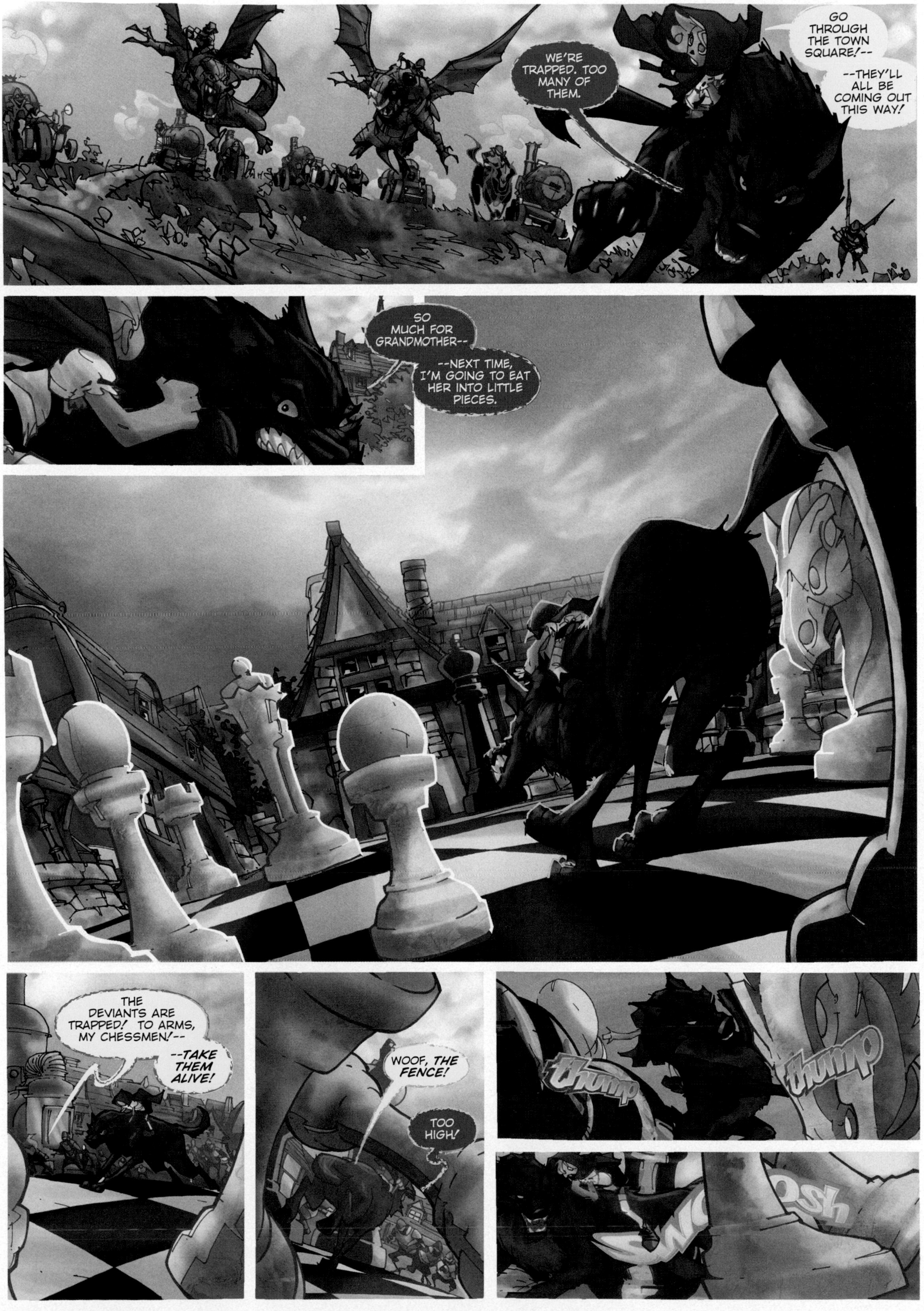
WE'RE TRAPPED. TOO MANY OF THEM.
GO THROUGH THE TOWN SQUARE!--
--THEY'LL ALL BE COMING OUT THIS WAY!
SO MUCH FOR GRANDMOTHER--
--NEXT TIME, I'M GOING TO EAT HER INTO LITTLE PIECES.
THE DEVIANTS ARE TRAPPED! TO ARMS, MY CHESSMEN!--
--TAKE THEM ALIVE!
WOOF, THE FENCE!
TOO HIGH!
thump
thump

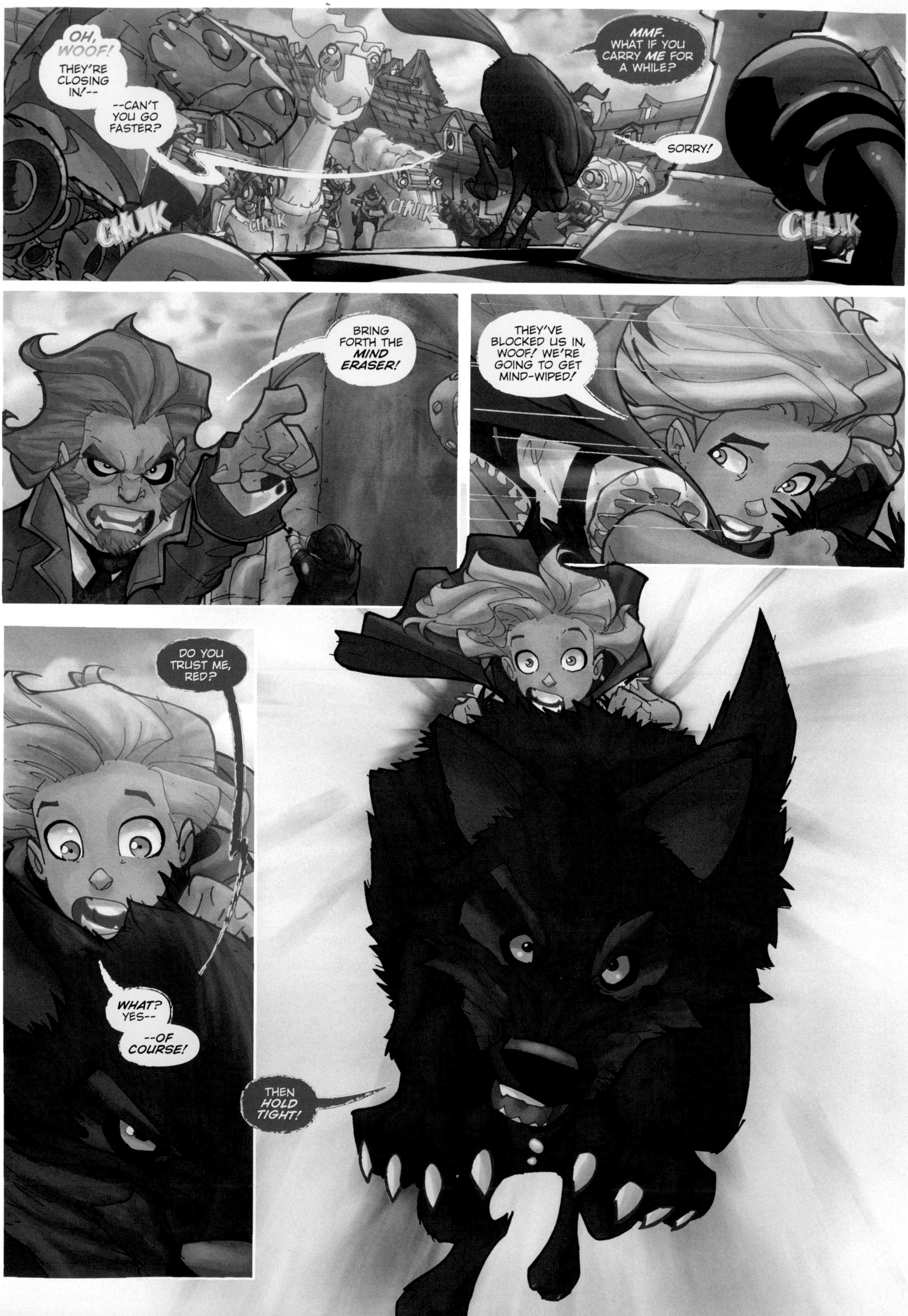
OH, WOOF! THEY'RE CLOSING IN!--
--CAN'T YOU GO FASTER?
MMF. WHAT IF YOU CARRY ME FOR A WHILE?
SORRY!
CHUK
CHUK
CHUK
CHUK
BRING FORTH THE MIND ERASER!
THEY'VE BLOCKED US IN, WOOF! WE'RE GOING TO GET MIND-WIPED!
DO YOU TRUST ME, RED?
WHAT? YES--
--OF COURSE!
THEN HOLD TIGHT!

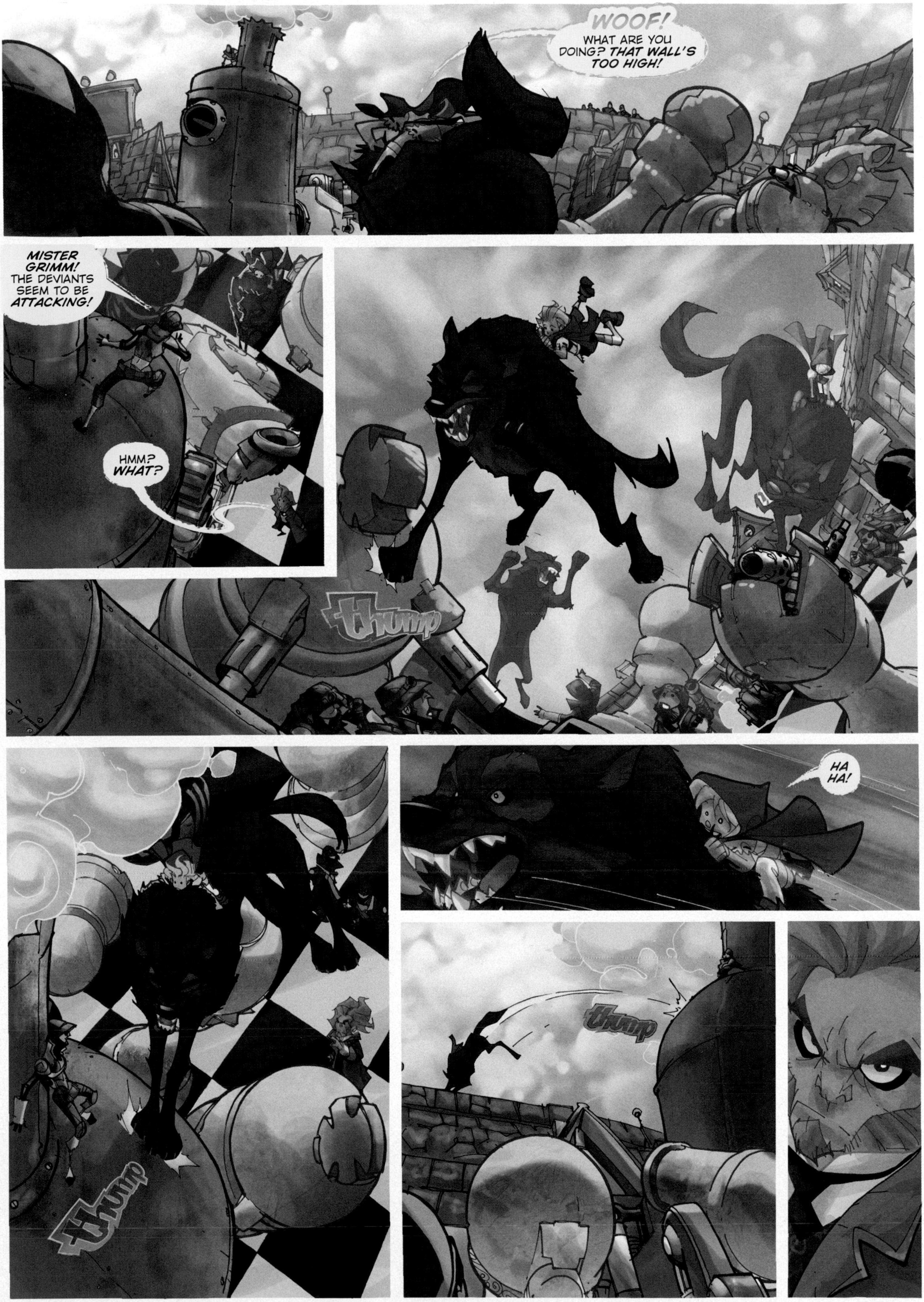
WOOF!
WHAT ARE YOU DOING? THAT WALL'S TOO HIGH!
MISTER GRIMM! THE DEVIANTS SEEM TO BE ATTACKING!
HMM? WHAT?
THUMP
HA HA!
THUMP
THUMP

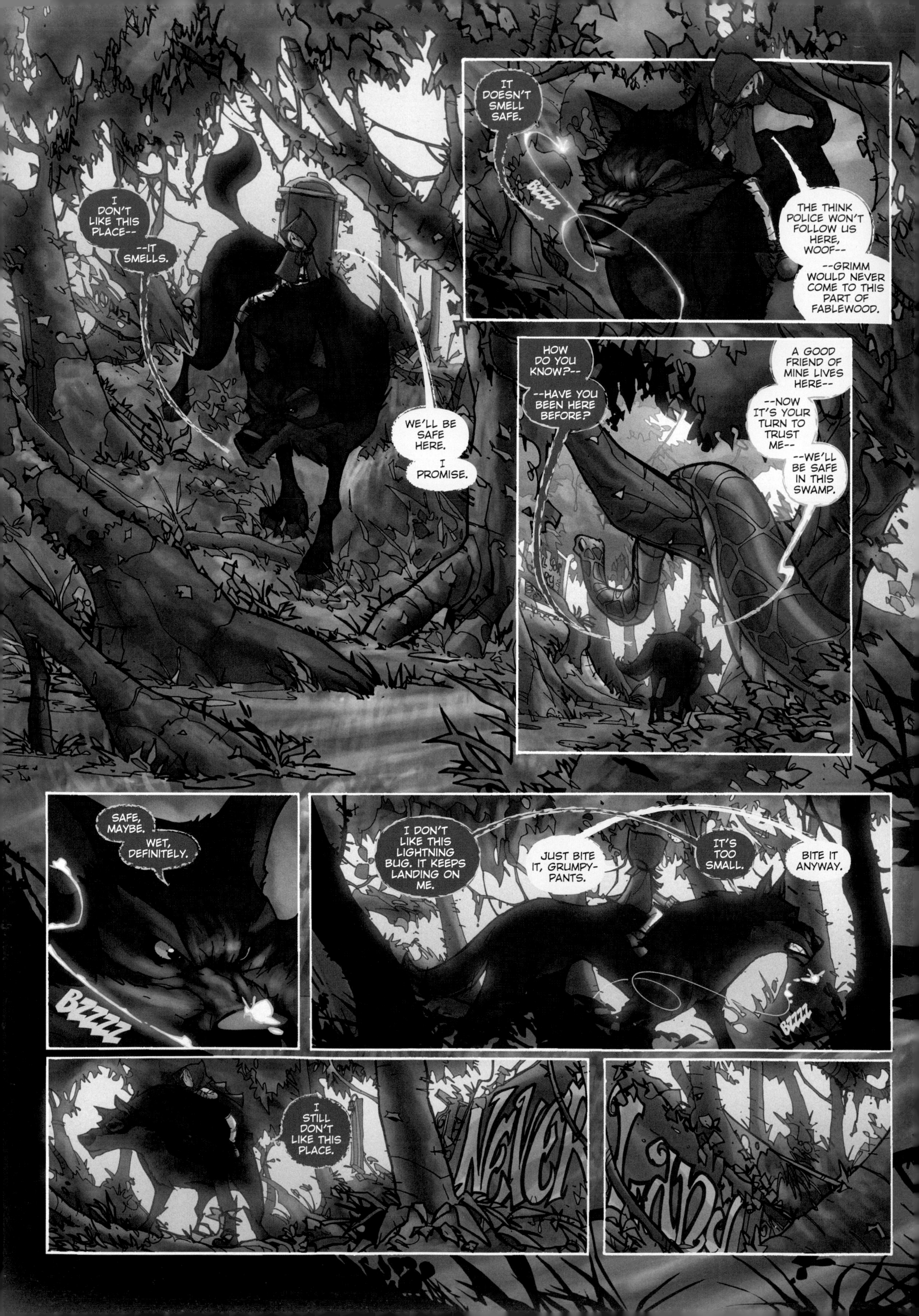

I DON'T LIKE THIS PLACE--
--IT SMELLS.
WE'LL BE SAFE HERE.
I PROMISE.
IT DOESN'T SMELL SAFE.
BZZZZ
THE THINK POLICE WON'T FOLLOW US HERE, WOOF--
--GRIMM WOULD NEVER COME TO THIS PART OF FABLEWOOD.
HOW DO YOU KNOW?--
--HAVE YOU BEEN HERE BEFORE?
A GOOD FRIEND OF MINE LIVES HERE--
--NOW IT'S YOUR TURN TO TRUST ME--
--WE'LL BE SAFE IN THIS SWAMP.
SAFE, MAYBE.
WET, DEFINITELY.
I DON'T LIKE THIS LIGHTNING BUG. IT KEEPS LANDING ON ME.
JUST BITE IT, GRUMPY-PANTS.
IT'S TOO SMALL.
BITE IT ANYWAY.
I STILL DON'T LIKE THIS PLACE.
NEVER

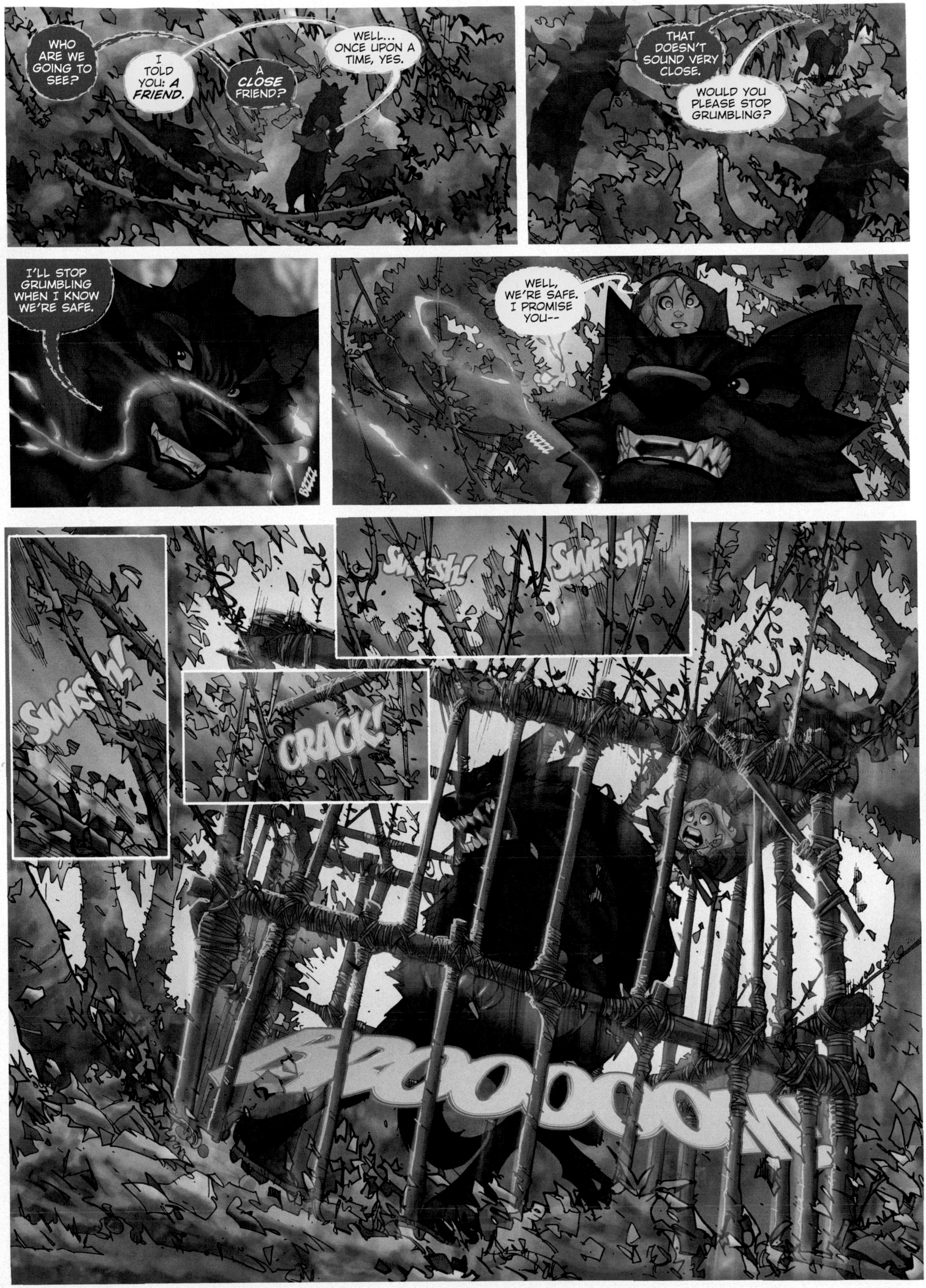

WHO ARE WE GOING TO SEE?
I TOLD YOU: *A FRIEND*.
A *CLOSE* FRIEND?
WELL... ONCE UPON A TIME, YES.
THAT DOESN'T SOUND VERY CLOSE.
WOULD YOU PLEASE STOP GRUMBLING?
I'LL STOP GRUMBLING WHEN I KNOW WE'RE SAFE.
BZZZZ
WELL, WE'RE SAFE. I PROMISE YOU--
BZZZZ
SWISH!
SWISH!
SWISH
CRACK!
BROOOOM!

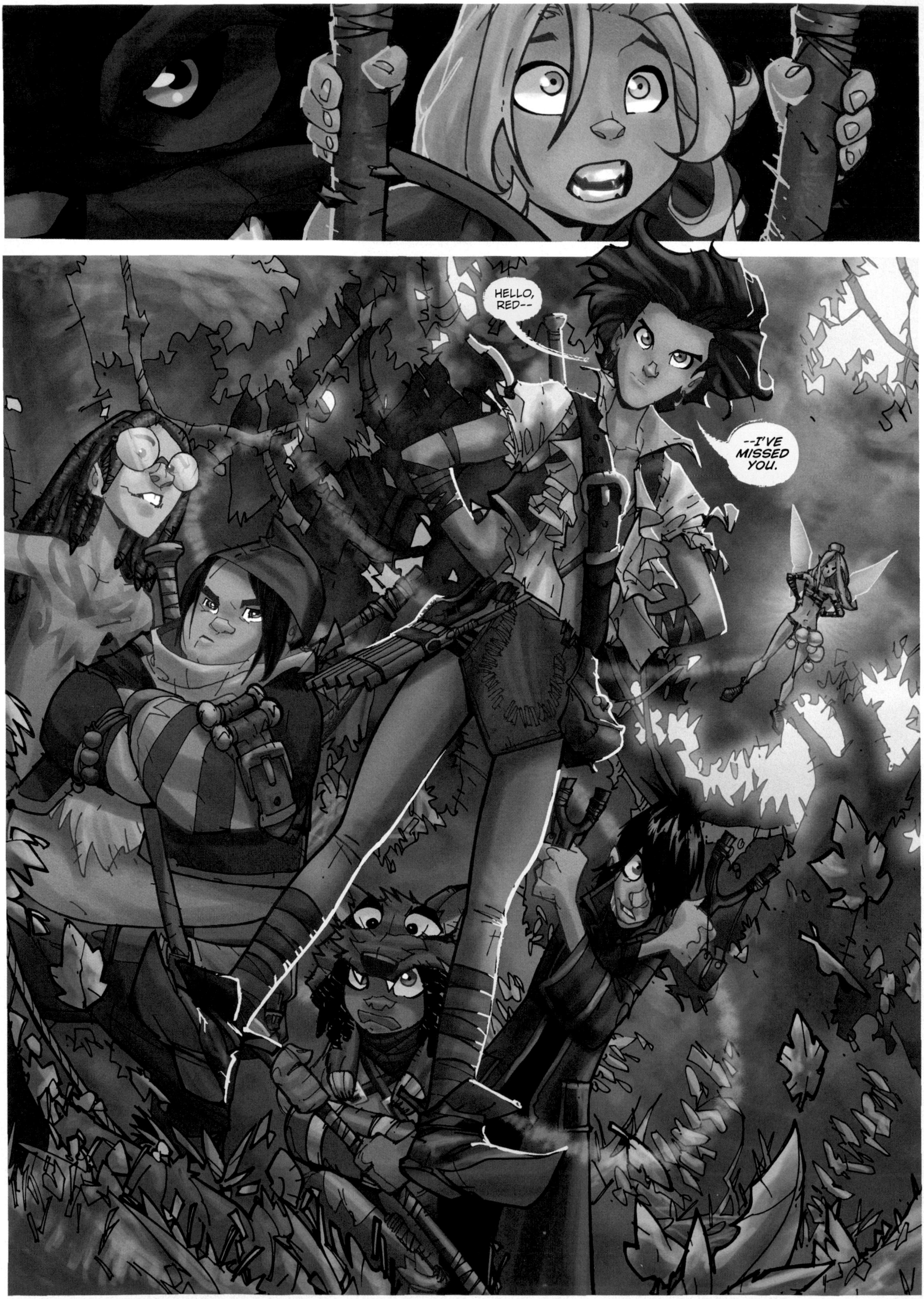
HELLO, RED--
--I'VE MISSED YOU.

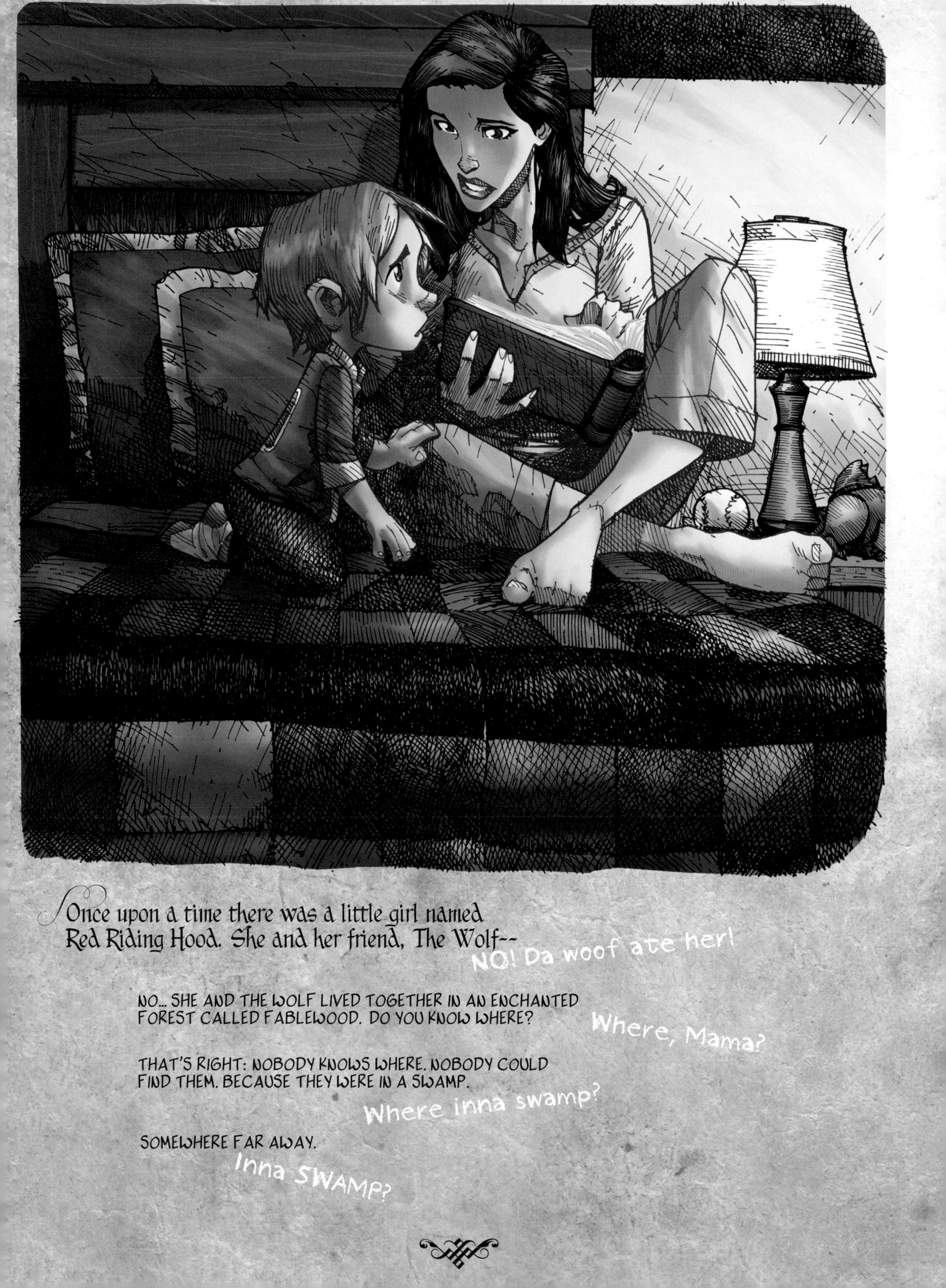

Once upon a time there was a little girl named Red Riding Hood. She and her friend, The Wolf--

NO! Da woof ate her!

NO... SHE AND THE WOLF LIVED TOGETHER IN AN ENCHANTED FOREST CALLED FABLEWOOD. DO YOU KNOW WHERE?

Where, Mama?

THAT'S RIGHT: NOBODY KNOWS WHERE. NOBODY COULD FIND THEM. BECAUSE THEY WERE IN A SWAMP.

Where inna swamp?

SOMEWHERE FAR AWAY.

Inna SWAMP?

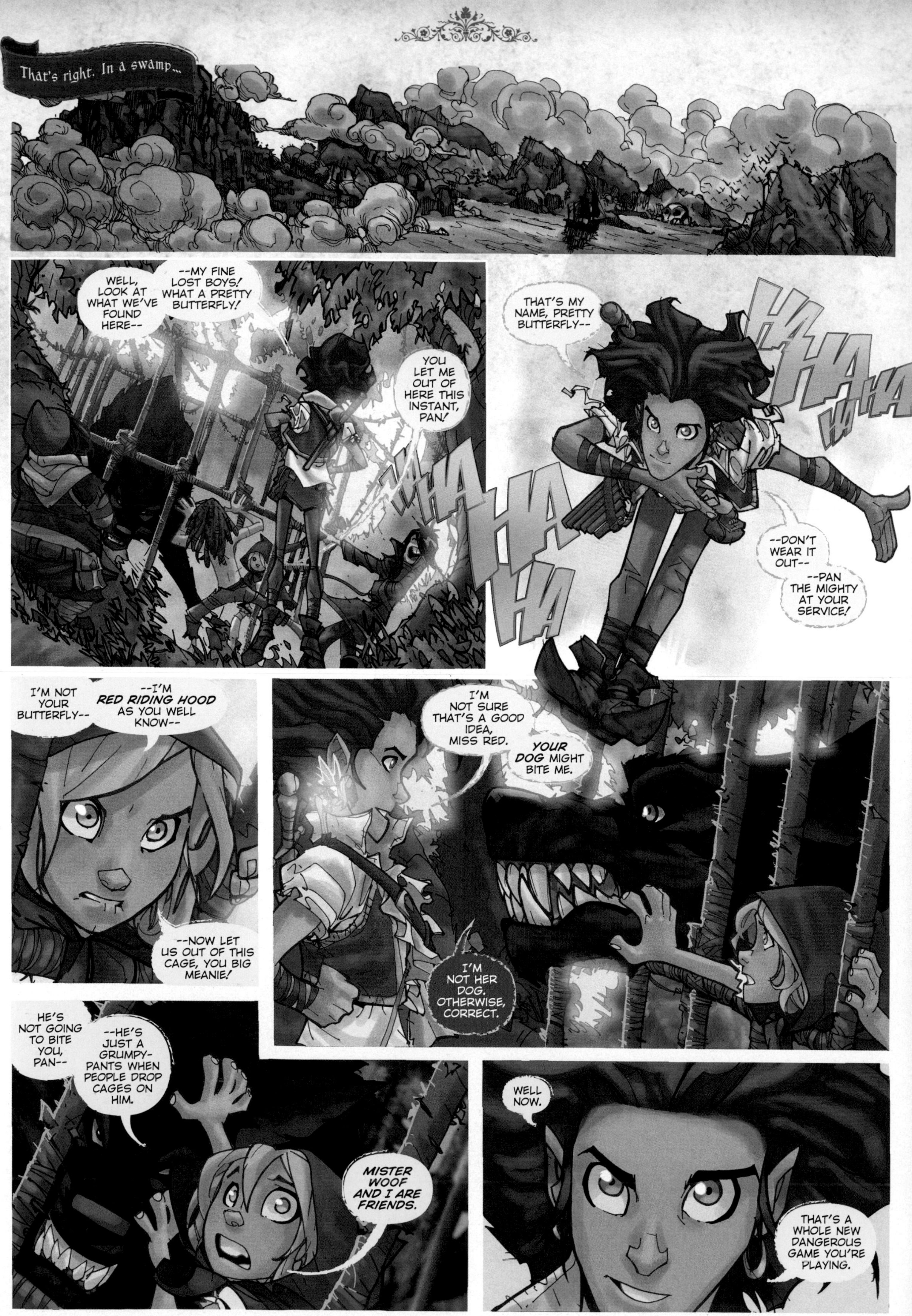

That's right. In a swamp...
WELL, LOOK AT WHAT WE'VE FOUND HERE--
--MY FINE LOST BOYS! WHAT A PRETTY BUTTERFLY!
YOU LET ME OUT OF HERE THIS INSTANT, PAN!
HA HA HA HA
THAT'S MY NAME, PRETTY BUTTERFLY--
HA HA HA HA
--DON'T WEAR IT OUT--
--PAN THE MIGHTY AT YOUR SERVICE!
I'M NOT YOUR BUTTERFLY--
--I'M **RED RIDING HOOD** AS YOU WELL KNOW--
--NOW LET US OUT OF THIS CAGE, YOU BIG MEANIE!
I'M NOT SURE THAT'S A GOOD IDEA, MISS RED. **YOUR DOG** MIGHT BITE ME.
I'M NOT HER DOG. OTHERWISE, CORRECT.
HE'S NOT GOING TO BITE YOU, PAN--
--HE'S JUST A GRUMPY-PANTS WHEN PEOPLE DROP CAGES ON HIM.
MISTER WOOF AND I ARE FRIENDS.
WELL NOW.
THAT'S A WHOLE NEW DANGEROUS GAME YOU'RE PLAYING.

SHE'S A SPY FOR THE THINK POLICE. I SAY WE FRY HER.

GIVE ME YOUR HAND.

WHY?

I WANT TO LOOK AT IT.

BAD IDEA, RED-- --I DON'T TRUST HIM.

THOSE WHO DON'T TRUST CAN'T BE TRUSTED, MISTER DOG. UNLIKE YOU, I PROMISE I WON'T BITE--

--NOW LET'S SEE HOW MUCH YOU TRUST *ME*, RED.

GOOD GIRL--

--NOW JUST FOR FUN, WHY DON'T YOU TELL US WHY YOU'VE COME ALL THE WAY TO OUR LITTLE CORNER OF THE SWAMP, UNANNOUNCED AND UNINVITED?

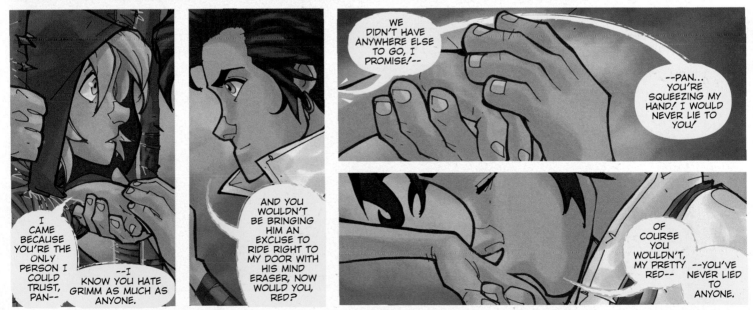

I CAME BECAUSE YOU'RE THE ONLY PERSON I COULD TRUST, PAN-- --I KNOW YOU HATE GRIMM AS MUCH AS ANYONE.

AND YOU WOULDN'T BE BRINGING HIM AN EXCUSE TO RIDE RIGHT TO MY DOOR WITH HIS MIND ERASER, NOW WOULD YOU, RED?

WE DIDN'T HAVE ANYWHERE ELSE TO GO, I PROMISE!--

--PAN... YOU'RE SQUEEZING MY HAND! I WOULD NEVER LIE TO YOU!

OF COURSE YOU WOULDN'T, MY PRETTY RED-- --YOU'VE NEVER LIED TO ANYONE.

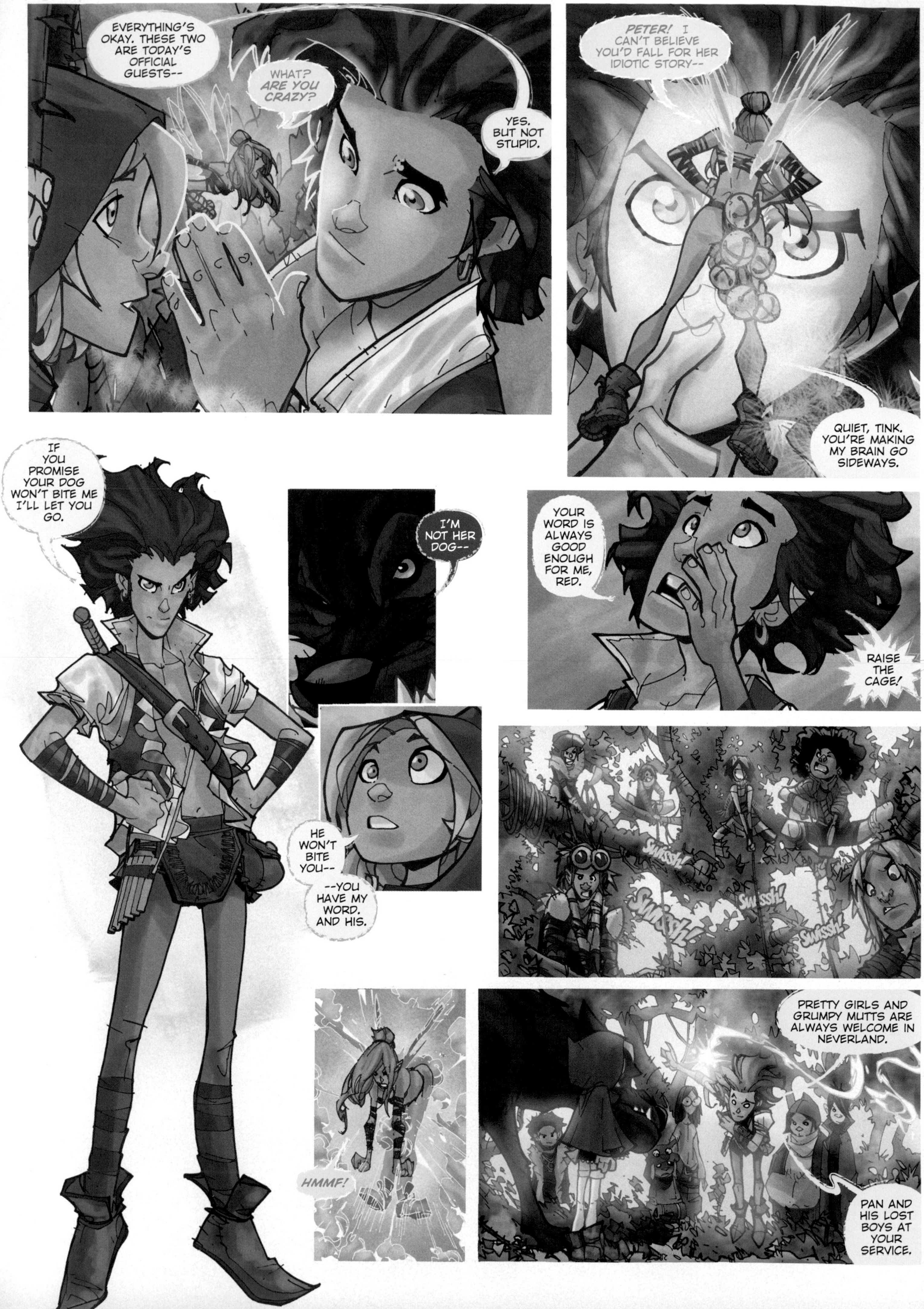
EVERYTHING'S OKAY. THESE TWO ARE TODAY'S OFFICIAL GUESTS--
WHAT? ARE YOU CRAZY?
YES. BUT NOT STUPID.
PETER! I CAN'T BELIEVE YOU'D FALL FOR HER IDIOTIC STORY--
QUIET, TINK. YOU'RE MAKING MY BRAIN GO SIDEWAYS.
IF YOU PROMISE YOUR DOG WON'T BITE ME I'LL LET YOU GO.
I'M NOT HER DOG--
HE WON'T BITE YOU--
--YOU HAVE MY WORD. AND HIS.
YOUR WORD IS ALWAYS GOOD ENOUGH FOR ME, RED.
RAISE THE CAGE!
SWISSH!
SWISSSH!
SWISSSH!
SWISSSH!
HMMF!
PRETTY GIRLS AND GRUMPY MUTTS ARE ALWAYS WELCOME IN NEVERLAND.
PAN AND HIS LOST BOYS AT YOUR SERVICE.

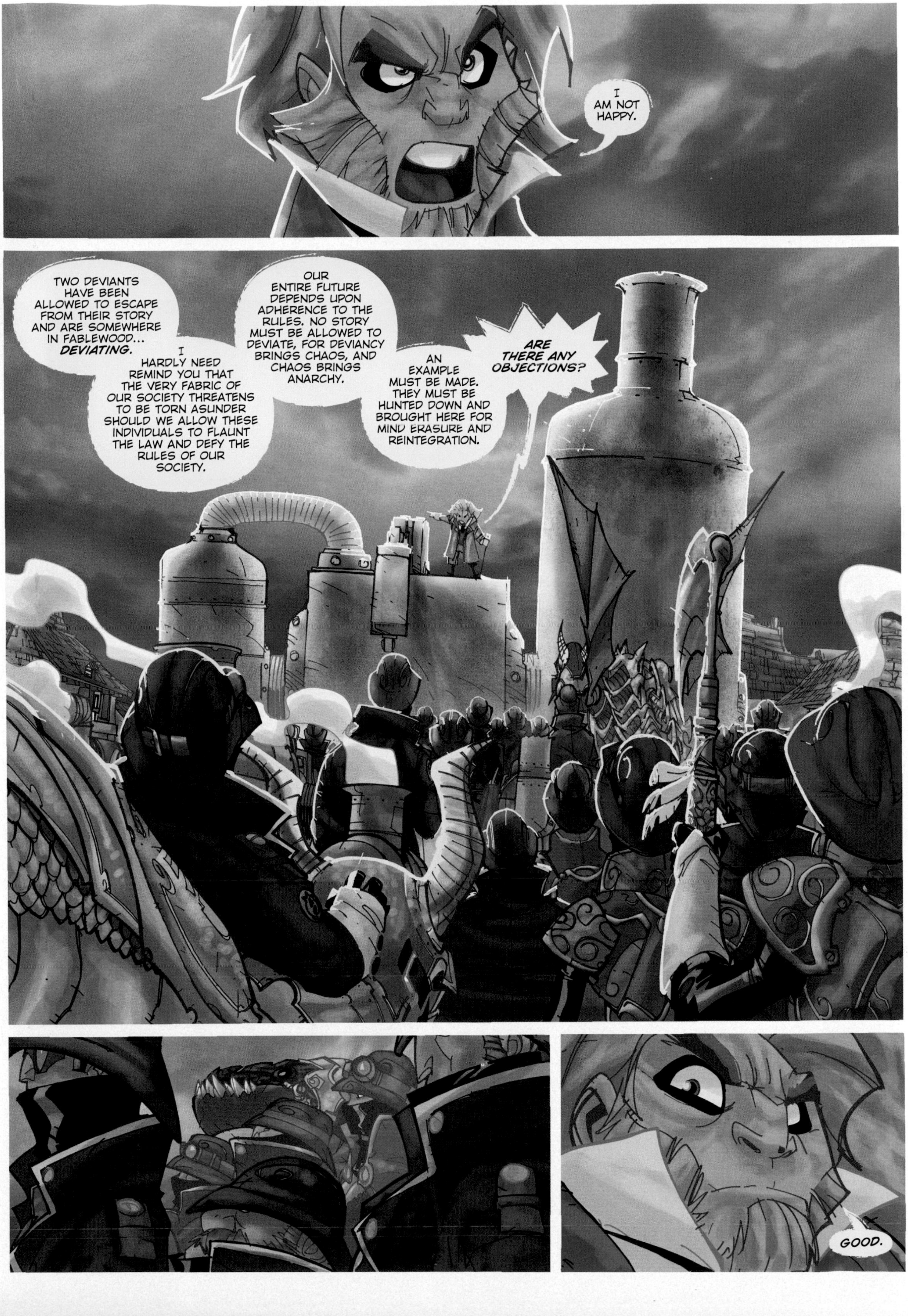
I AM NOT HAPPY.
TWO DEVIANTS HAVE BEEN ALLOWED TO ESCAPE FROM THEIR STORY AND ARE SOMEWHERE IN FABLEWOOD... *DEVIATING.*
I HARDLY NEED REMIND YOU THAT THE VERY FABRIC OF OUR SOCIETY THREATENS TO BE TORN ASUNDER SHOULD WE ALLOW THESE INDIVIDUALS TO FLAUNT THE LAW AND DEFY THE RULES OF OUR SOCIETY.
OUR ENTIRE FUTURE DEPENDS UPON ADHERENCE TO THE RULES. NO STORY MUST BE ALLOWED TO DEVIATE, FOR DEVIANCY BRINGS CHAOS, AND CHAOS BRINGS ANARCHY.
AN EXAMPLE MUST BE MADE. THEY MUST BE HUNTED DOWN AND BROUGHT HERE FOR MIND ERASURE AND REINTEGRATION.
ARE THERE ANY OBJECTIONS?
GOOD.

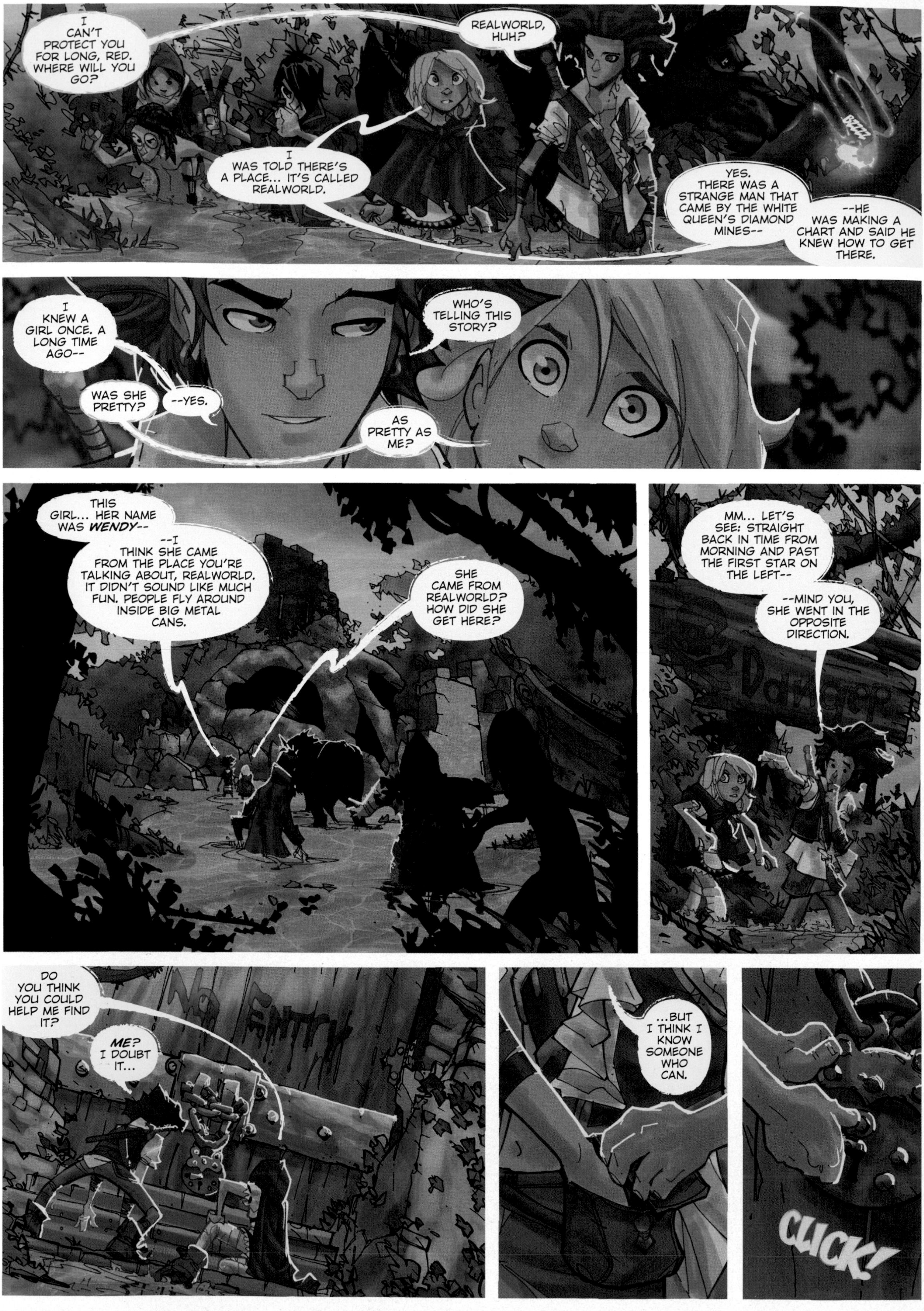
I CAN'T PROTECT YOU FOR LONG, RED. WHERE WILL YOU GO?
REALWORLD, HUH?
I WAS TOLD THERE'S A PLACE... IT'S CALLED REALWORLD.
YES. THERE WAS A STRANGE MAN THAT CAME BY THE WHITE QUEEN'S DIAMOND MINES--
--HE WAS MAKING A CHART AND SAID HE KNEW HOW TO GET THERE.
I KNEW A GIRL ONCE. A LONG TIME AGO--
WHO'S TELLING THIS STORY?
WAS SHE PRETTY?
--YES.
AS PRETTY AS ME?
THIS GIRL... HER NAME WAS *WENDY*--
--I THINK SHE CAME FROM THE PLACE YOU'RE TALKING ABOUT, REALWORLD. IT DIDN'T SOUND LIKE MUCH FUN. PEOPLE FLY AROUND INSIDE BIG METAL CANS.
SHE CAME FROM REALWORLD? HOW DID SHE GET HERE?
MM... LET'S SEE: STRAIGHT BACK IN TIME FROM MORNING AND PAST THE FIRST STAR ON THE LEFT--
--MIND YOU, SHE WENT IN THE OPPOSITE DIRECTION.
DANGER
NO ENTRY
DO YOU THINK YOU COULD HELP ME FIND IT?
ME? I DOUBT IT...
...BUT I THINK I KNOW SOMEONE WHO CAN.
CLICK!

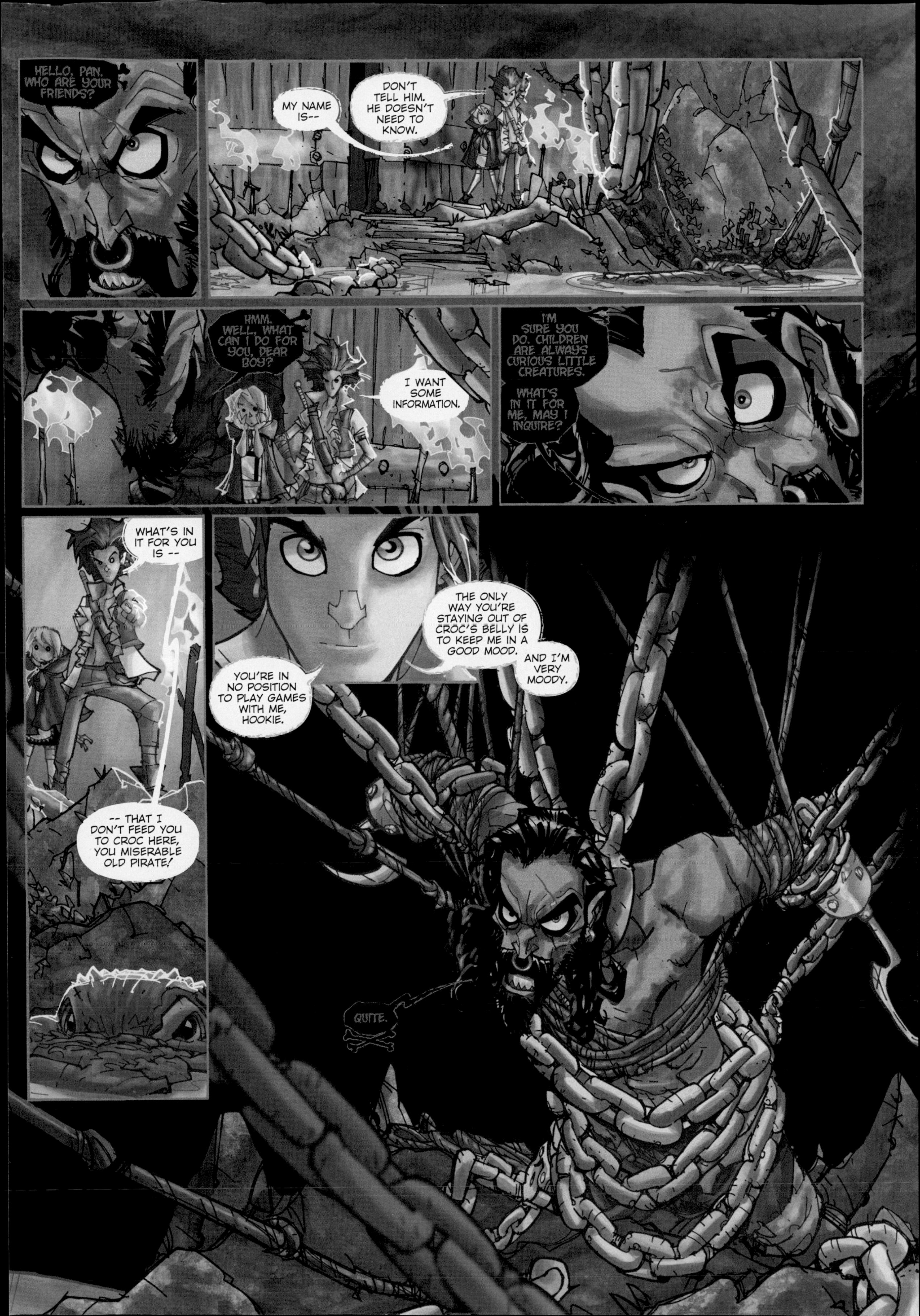
HELLO, PAN. WHO ARE YOUR FRIENDS?
MY NAME IS--
DON'T TELL HIM. HE DOESN'T NEED TO KNOW.
HMM. WELL, WHAT CAN I DO FOR YOU, DEAR BOY?
I WANT SOME INFORMATION.
I'M SURE YOU DO. CHILDREN ARE ALWAYS CURIOUS LITTLE CREATURES.
WHAT'S IN IT FOR ME, MAY I INQUIRE?
WHAT'S IN IT FOR YOU IS --
-- THAT I DON'T FEED YOU TO CROC HERE, YOU MISERABLE OLD PIRATE!
YOU'RE IN NO POSITION TO PLAY GAMES WITH ME, HOOKIE.
THE ONLY WAY YOU'RE STAYING OUT OF CROC'S BELLY IS TO KEEP ME IN A GOOD MOOD.
AND I'M VERY MOODY.
QUITE.

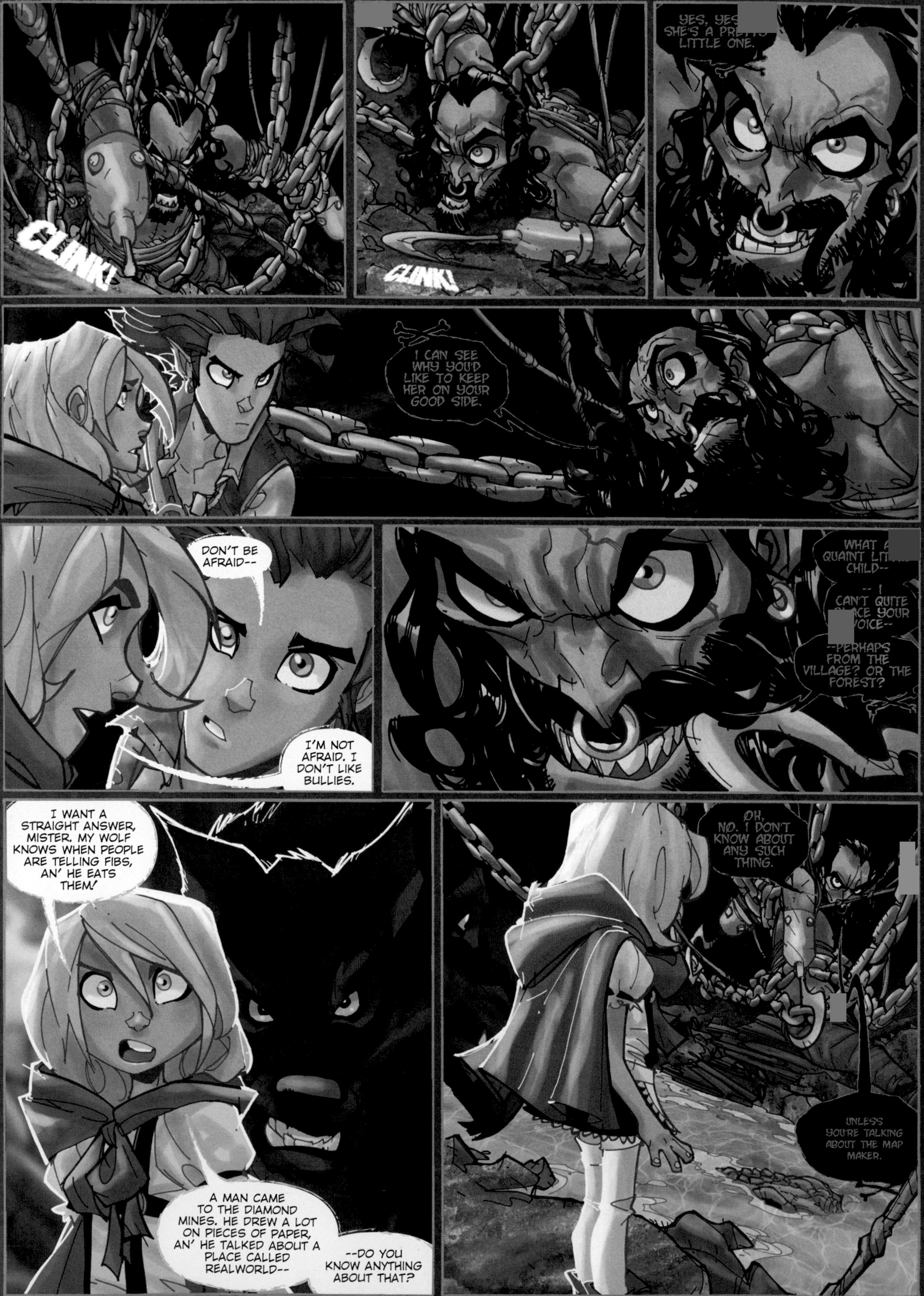
CLINK!
CLINK!
YES, YES SHE'S A PRE LITTLE ONE.
I CAN SEE WHY YOU'D LIKE TO KEEP HER ON YOUR GOOD SIDE.
DON'T BE AFRAID--
I'M NOT AFRAID. I DON'T LIKE BULLIES.
WHAT A QUAINT LIT CHILD--
-- I CAN'T QUITE ACE YOUR VOICE--
--PERHAPS FROM THE VILLAGE? OR THE FOREST?
I WANT A STRAIGHT ANSWER, MISTER. MY WOLF KNOWS WHEN PEOPLE ARE TELLING FIBS, AN' HE EATS THEM!
A MAN CAME TO THE DIAMOND MINES. HE DREW A LOT ON PIECES OF PAPER, AN' HE TALKED ABOUT A PLACE CALLED REALWORLD--
--DO YOU KNOW ANYTHING ABOUT THAT?
OH, NO. I DON'T KNOW ABOUT ANY SUCH THING.
UNLESS YOU'RE TALKING ABOUT THE MAP MAKER.

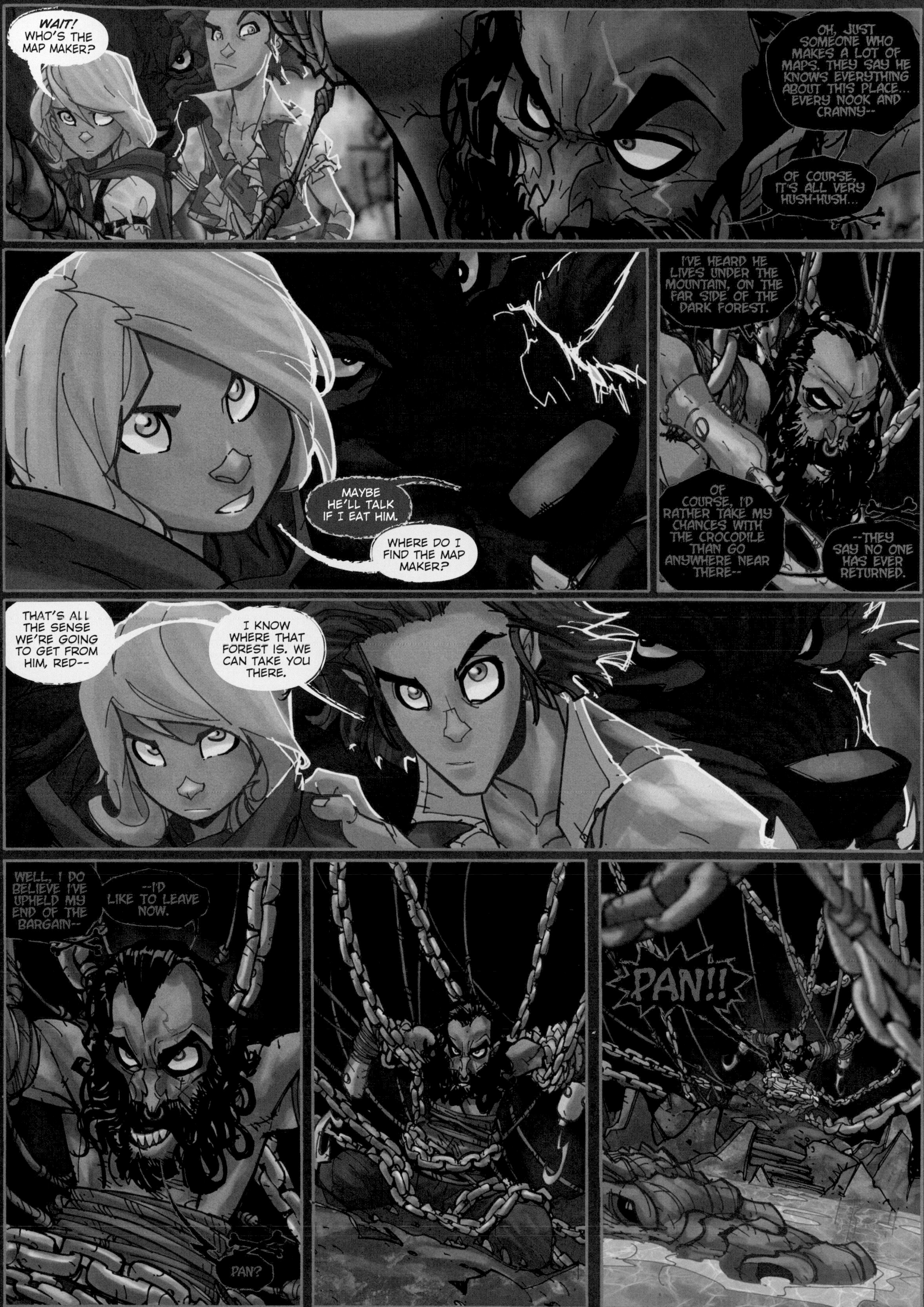
WAIT! WHO'S THE MAP MAKER?
OH, JUST SOMEONE WHO MAKES A LOT OF MAPS. THEY SAY HE KNOWS EVERYTHING ABOUT THIS PLACE... EVERY NOOK AND CRANNY--
OF COURSE, IT'S ALL VERY HUSH-HUSH...
MAYBE HE'LL TALK IF I EAT HIM.
WHERE DO I FIND THE MAP MAKER?
I'VE HEARD HE LIVES UNDER THE MOUNTAIN, ON THE FAR SIDE OF THE DARK FOREST.
OF COURSE, I'D RATHER TAKE MY CHANCES WITH THE CROCODILE THAN GO ANYWHERE NEAR THERE--
--THEY SAY NO ONE HAS EVER RETURNED.
THAT'S ALL THE SENSE WE'RE GOING TO GET FROM HIM, RED--
I KNOW WHERE THAT FOREST IS. WE CAN TAKE YOU THERE.
WELL, I DO BELIEVE I'VE UPHELD MY END OF THE BARGAIN--
--I'D LIKE TO LEAVE NOW.
PAN?
PAN!!

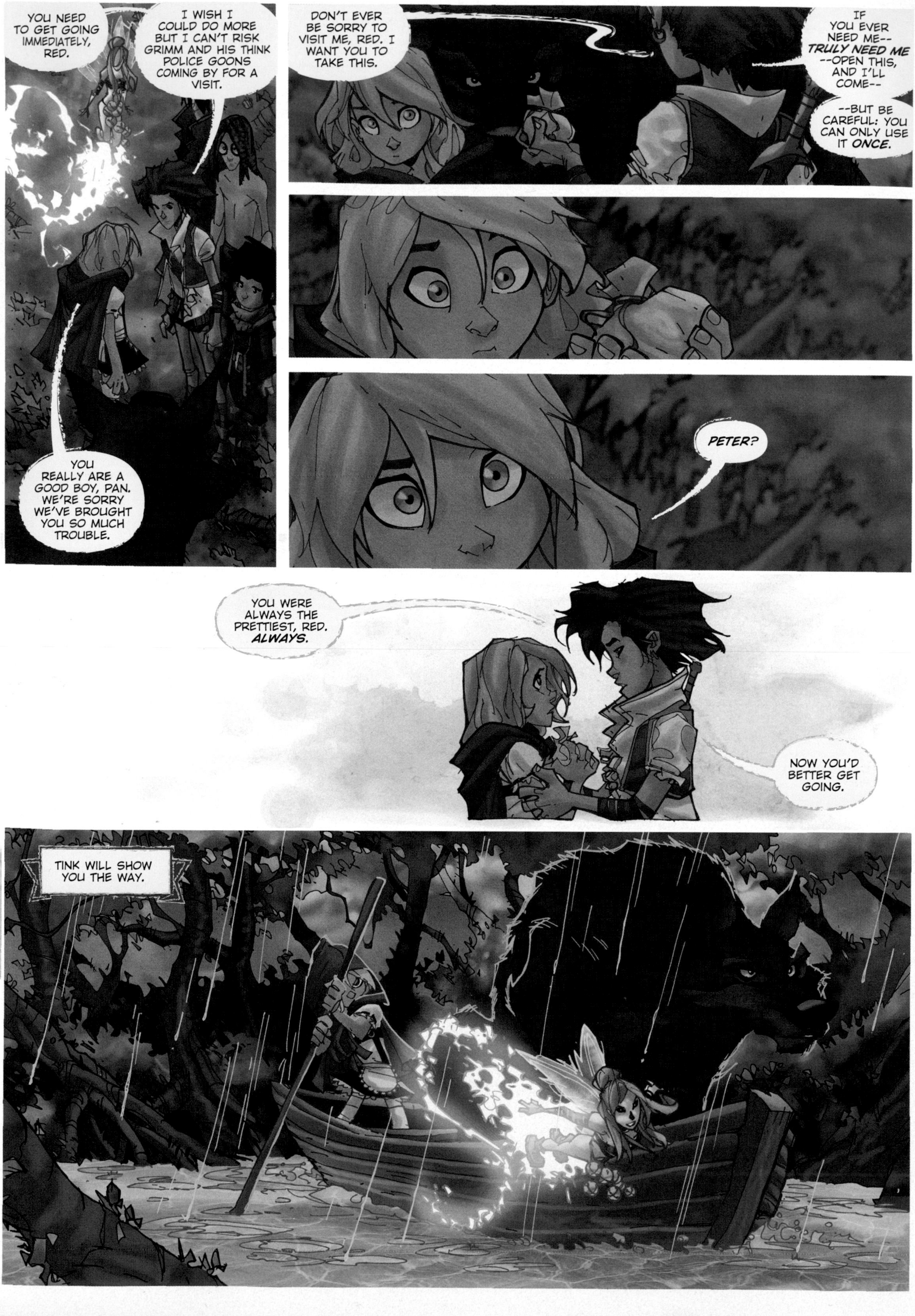

YOU NEED TO GET GOING IMMEDIATELY, RED.
I WISH I COULD DO MORE BUT I CAN'T RISK GRIMM AND HIS THINK POLICE GOONS COMING BY FOR A VISIT.
YOU REALLY ARE A GOOD BOY, PAN. WE'RE SORRY WE'VE BROUGHT YOU SO MUCH TROUBLE.
DON'T EVER BE SORRY TO VISIT ME, RED. I WANT YOU TO TAKE THIS.
IF YOU EVER NEED ME-- TRULY NEED ME --OPEN THIS, AND I'LL COME--
--BUT BE CAREFUL: YOU CAN ONLY USE IT ONCE.
PETER?
YOU WERE ALWAYS THE PRETTIEST, RED. ALWAYS.
NOW YOU'D BETTER GET GOING.
TINK WILL SHOW YOU THE WAY.

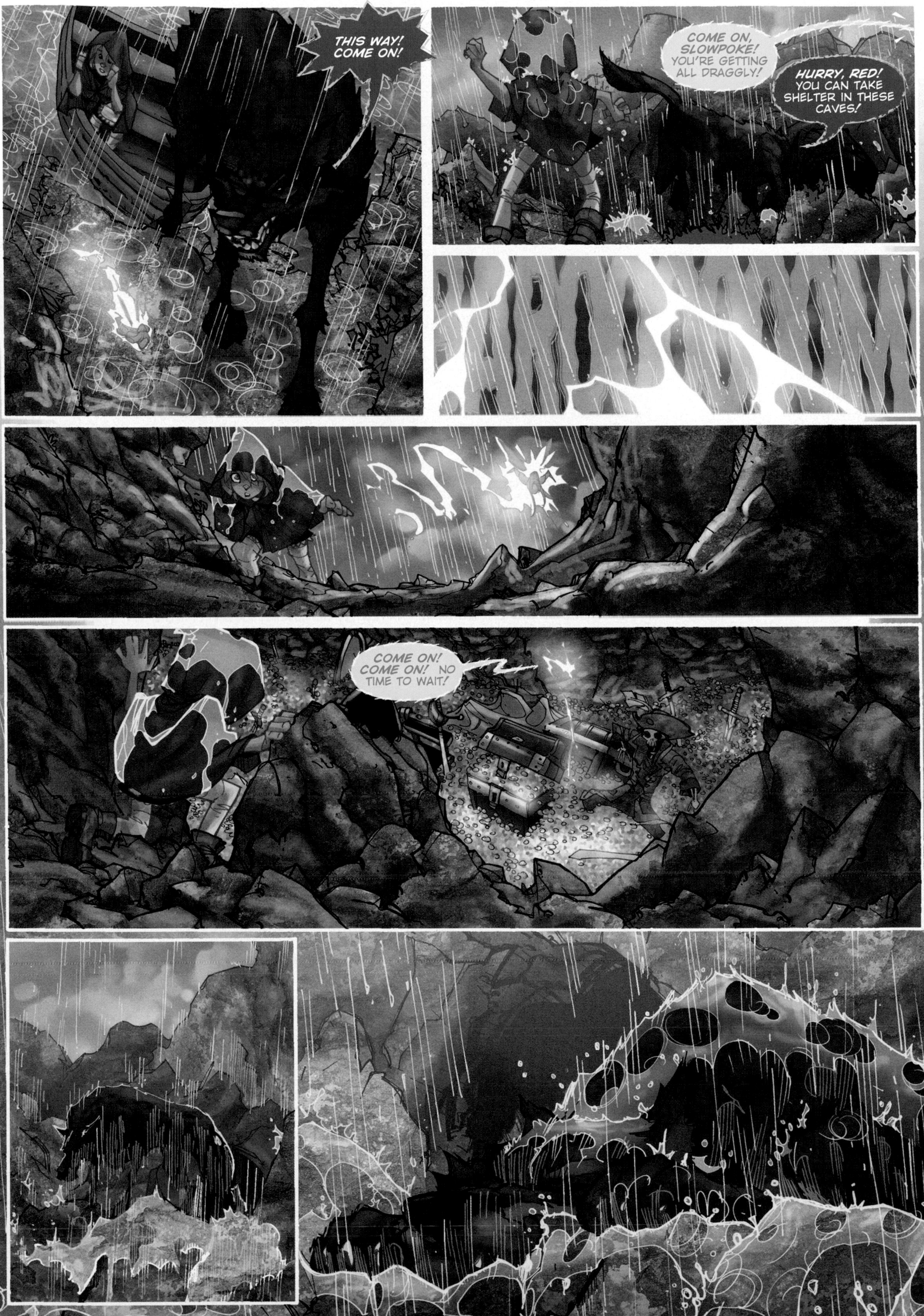
THIS WAY! COME ON!
COME ON, SLOWPOKE! YOU'RE GETTING ALL DRAGGLY!
HURRY, RED! YOU CAN TAKE SHELTER IN THESE CAVES!
COME ON! COME ON! NO TIME TO WAIT!

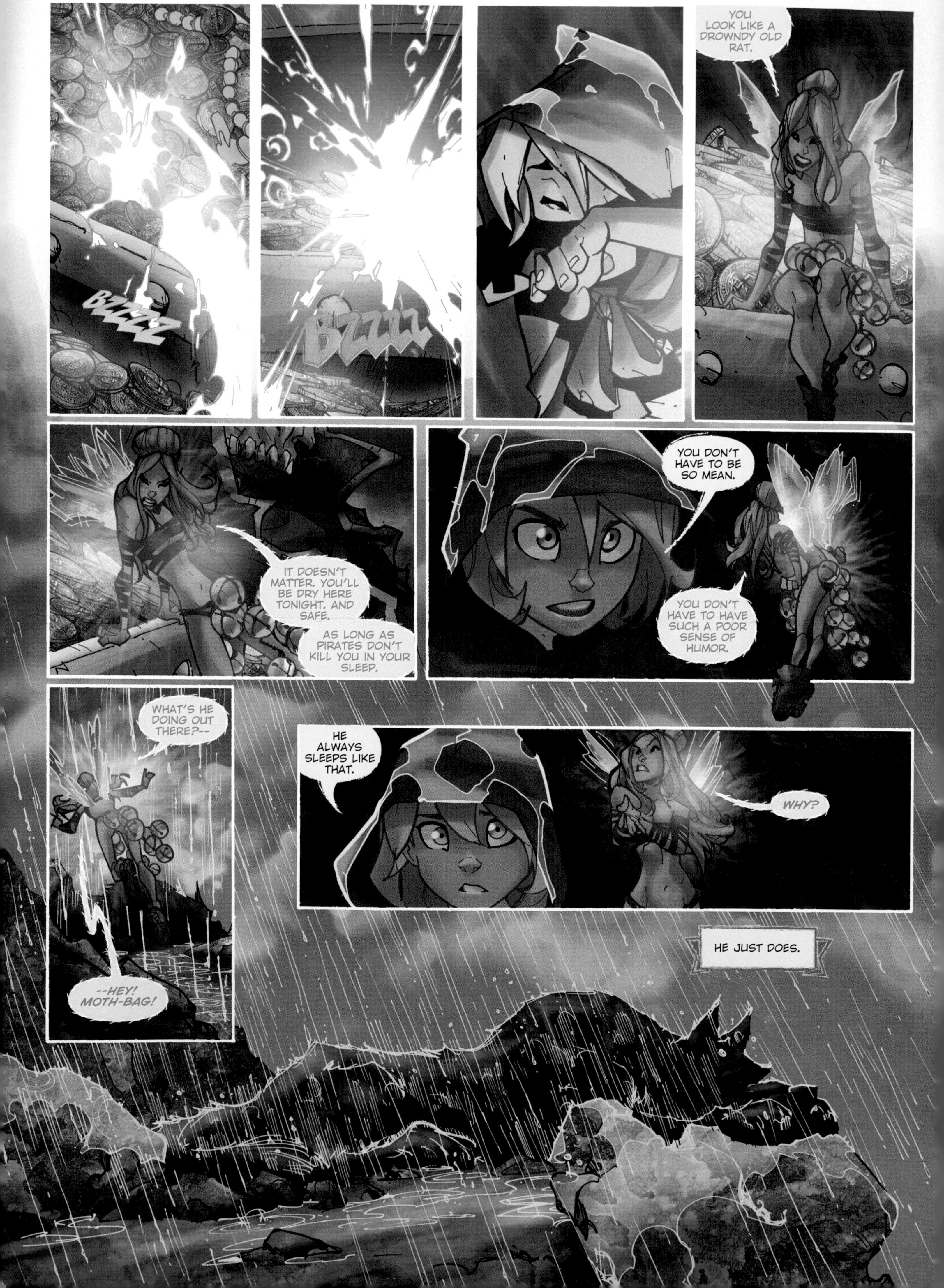
BZZZZ
BZZZZ
YOU LOOK LIKE A DROWNDY OLD RAT.
IT DOESN'T MATTER. YOU'LL BE DRY HERE TONIGHT. AND SAFE.
AS LONG AS PIRATES DON'T KILL YOU IN YOUR SLEEP.
YOU DON'T HAVE TO BE SO MEAN.
YOU DON'T HAVE TO HAVE SUCH A POOR SENSE OF HUMOR.
WHAT'S HE DOING OUT THERE?--
--HEY! MOTH-BAG!
HE ALWAYS SLEEPS LIKE THAT.
WHY?
HE JUST DOES.

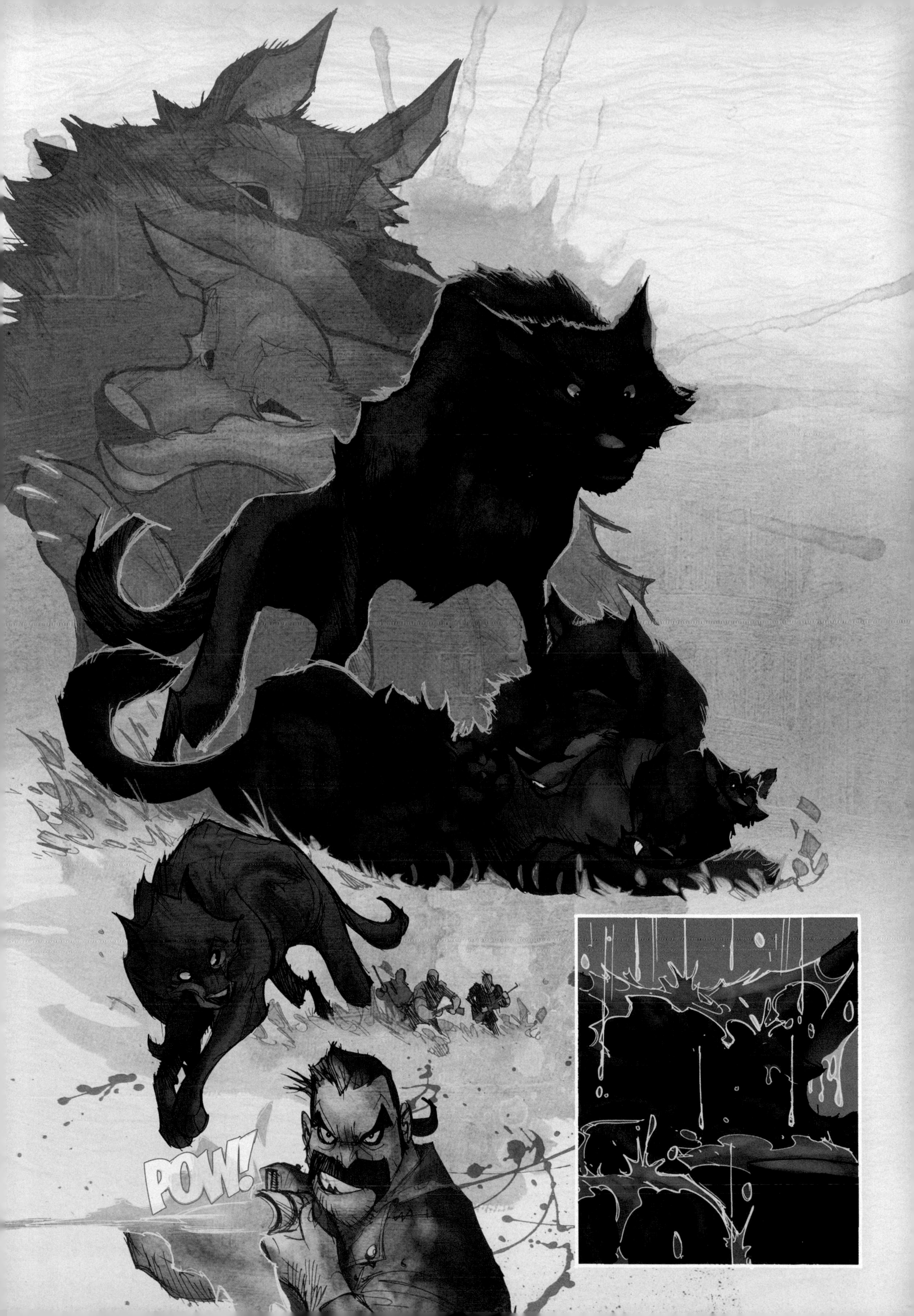
POW!

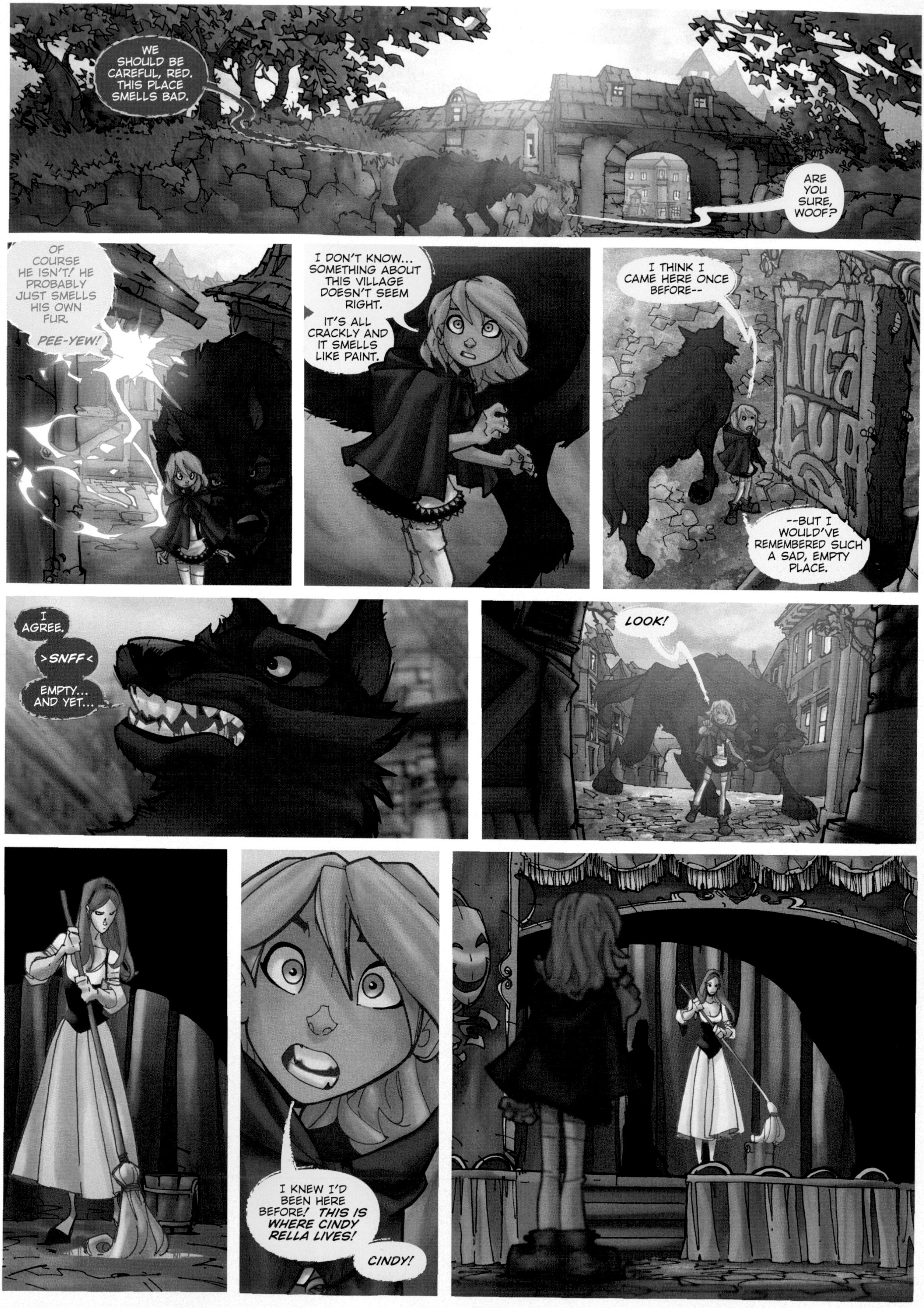
WE SHOULD BE CAREFUL, RED. THIS PLACE SMELLS BAD.
ARE YOU SURE, WOOF?
OF COURSE HE ISN'T! HE PROBABLY JUST SMELLS HIS OWN FUR.
PEE-YEW!
I DON'T KNOW... SOMETHING ABOUT THIS VILLAGE DOESN'T SEEM RIGHT.
IT'S ALL CRACKLY AND IT SMELLS LIKE PAINT.
I THINK I CAME HERE ONCE BEFORE--
--BUT I WOULD'VE REMEMBERED SUCH A SAD, EMPTY PLACE.
I AGREE.
>SNFF<
EMPTY... AND YET...
LOOK!
I KNEW I'D BEEN HERE BEFORE! THIS IS WHERE CINDY RELLA LIVES!
CINDY!

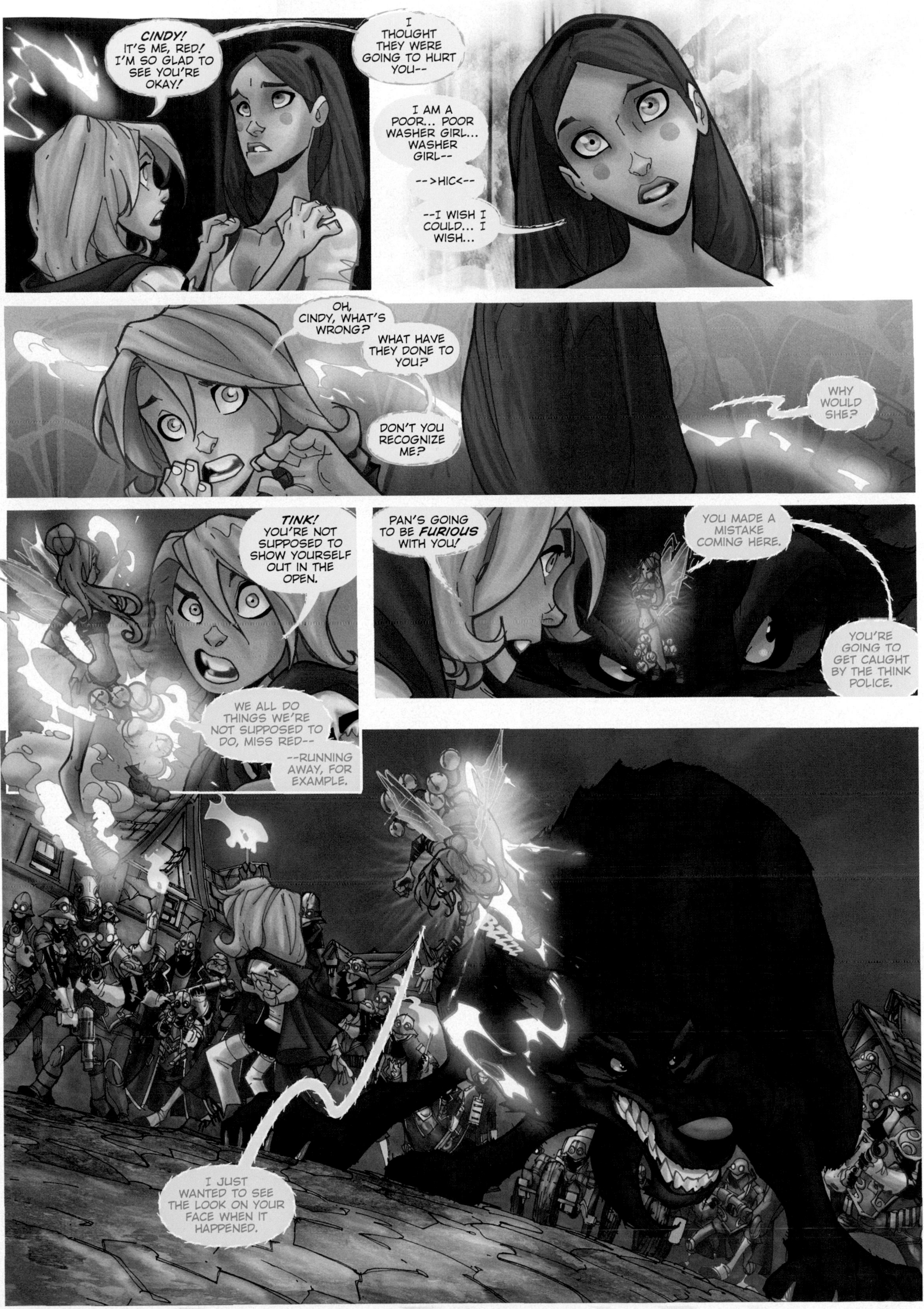

CINDY! IT'S ME, RED! I'M SO GLAD TO SEE YOU'RE OKAY!
I THOUGHT THEY WERE GOING TO HURT YOU--
I AM A POOR... POOR WASHER GIRL... WASHER GIRL--
-->HIC<--
--I WISH I COULD... I WISH...
OH, CINDY, WHAT'S WRONG?
WHAT HAVE THEY DONE TO YOU?
DON'T YOU RECOGNIZE ME?
WHY WOULD SHE?
TINK! YOU'RE NOT SUPPOSED TO SHOW YOURSELF OUT IN THE OPEN.
WE ALL DO THINGS WE'RE NOT SUPPOSED TO DO, MISS RED--
--RUNNING AWAY, FOR EXAMPLE.
PAN'S GOING TO BE FURIOUS WITH YOU!
YOU MADE A MISTAKE COMING HERE.
YOU'RE GOING TO GET CAUGHT BY THE THINK POLICE.
I JUST WANTED TO SEE THE LOOK ON YOUR FACE WHEN IT HAPPENED.

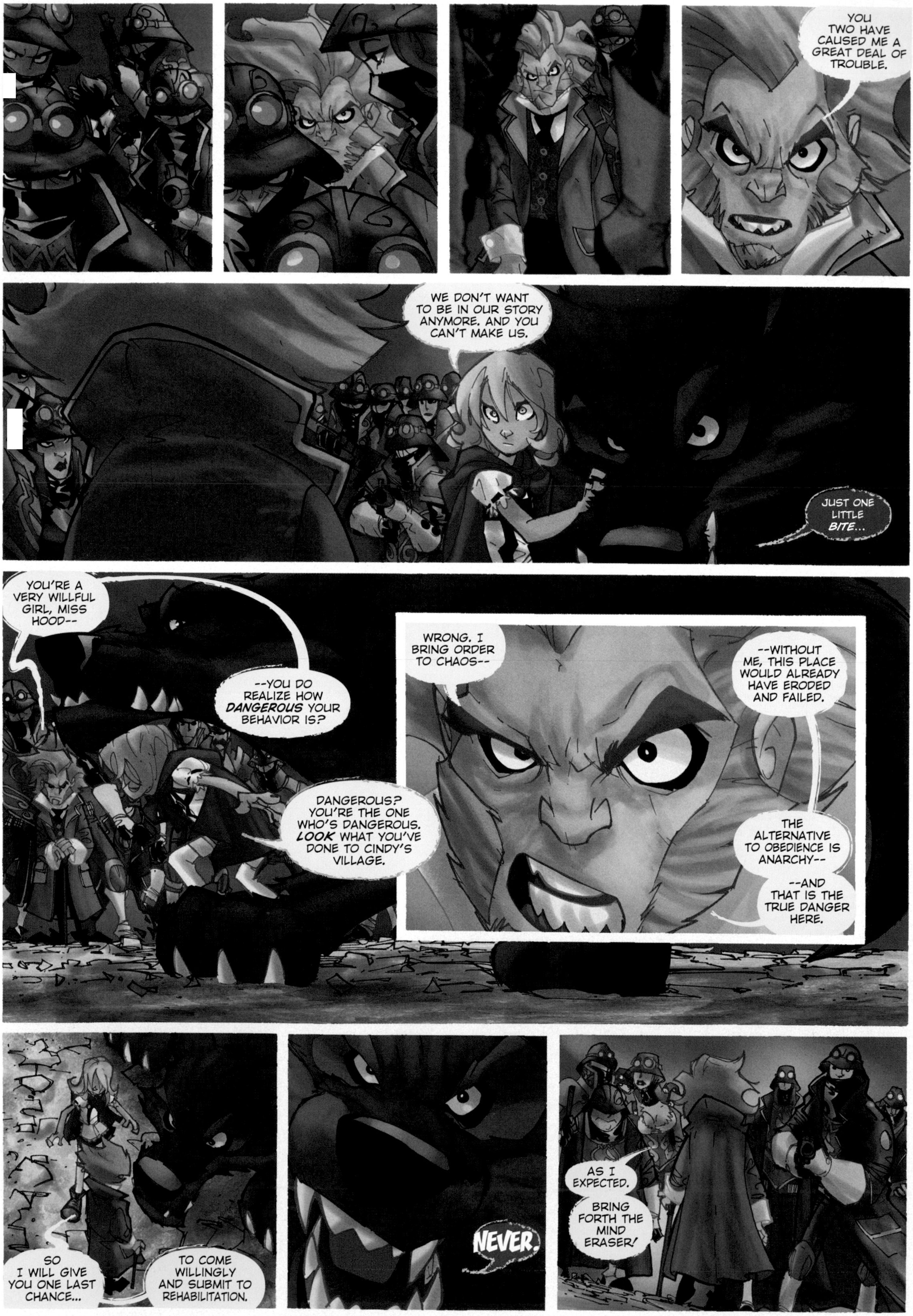

YOU TWO HAVE CAUSED ME A GREAT DEAL OF TROUBLE.
WE DON'T WANT TO BE IN OUR STORY ANYMORE. AND YOU CAN'T MAKE US.
JUST ONE LITTLE *BITE*...
YOU'RE A VERY WILLFUL GIRL, MISS HOOD--
--YOU DO REALIZE HOW *DANGEROUS* YOUR BEHAVIOR IS?
DANGEROUS? YOU'RE THE ONE WHO'S DANGEROUS. *LOOK* WHAT YOU'VE DONE TO CINDY'S VILLAGE.
WRONG. I BRING ORDER TO CHAOS--
--WITHOUT ME, THIS PLACE WOULD ALREADY HAVE ERODED AND FAILED.
THE ALTERNATIVE TO OBEDIENCE IS ANARCHY--
--AND THAT IS THE TRUE DANGER HERE.
SO I WILL GIVE YOU ONE LAST CHANCE...
TO COME WILLINGLY AND SUBMIT TO REHABILITATION.
NEVER.
AS I EXPECTED.
BRING FORTH THE MIND ERASER!

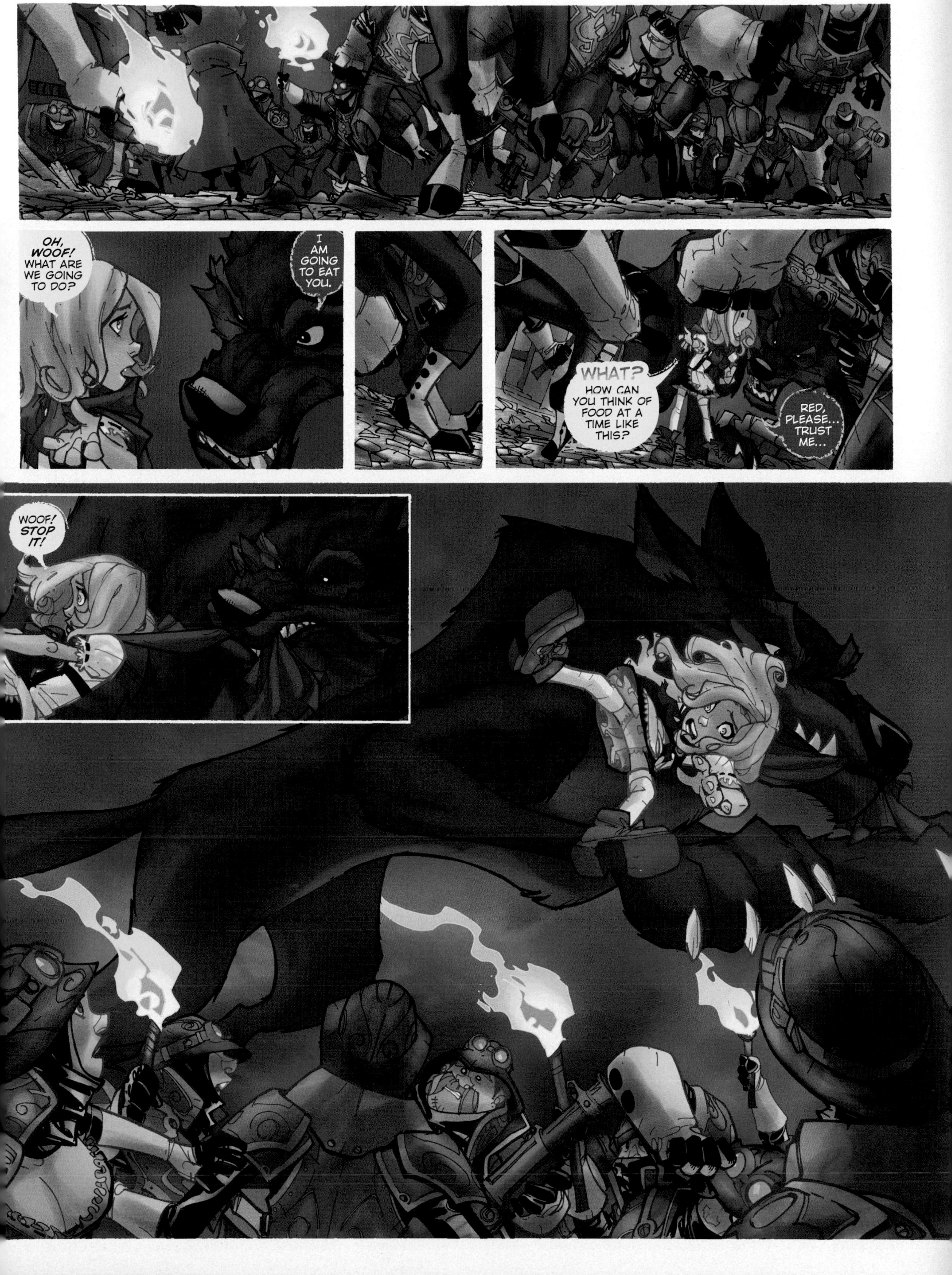
OH, WOOF! WHAT ARE WE GOING TO DO?
I AM GOING TO EAT YOU.
WHAT? HOW CAN YOU THINK OF FOOD AT A TIME LIKE THIS?
RED, PLEASE... TRUST ME...
WOOF! STOP IT!

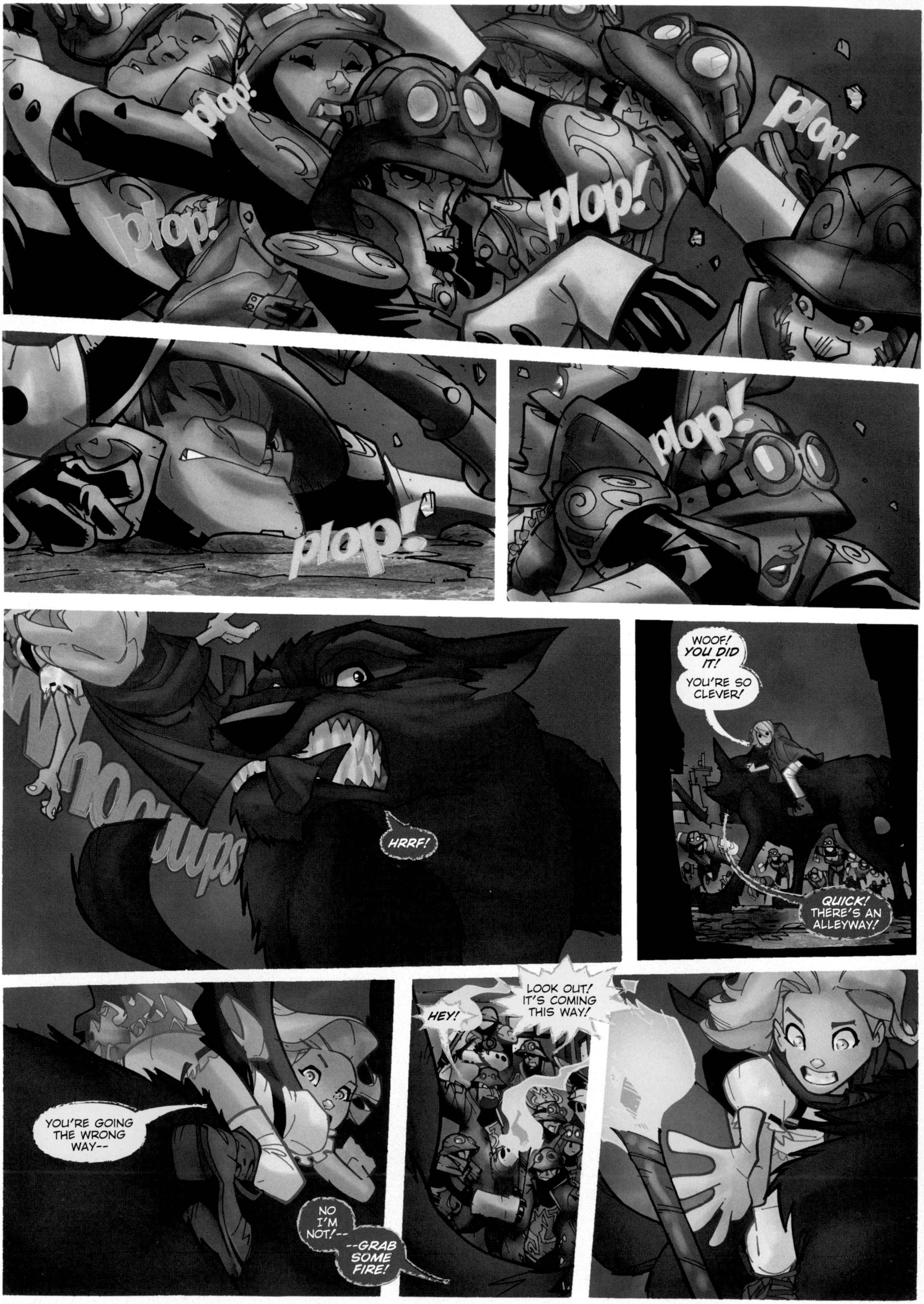
plop!
plop!
plop!
plop!
plop!
plop!
Whooops
HRRF!
WOOF! YOU DID IT!
YOU'RE SO CLEVER!
QUICK! THERE'S AN ALLEYWAY!
YOU'RE GOING THE WRONG WAY--
NO I'M NOT!--
--GRAB SOME FIRE!
HEY!
LOOK OUT! IT'S COMING THIS WAY!

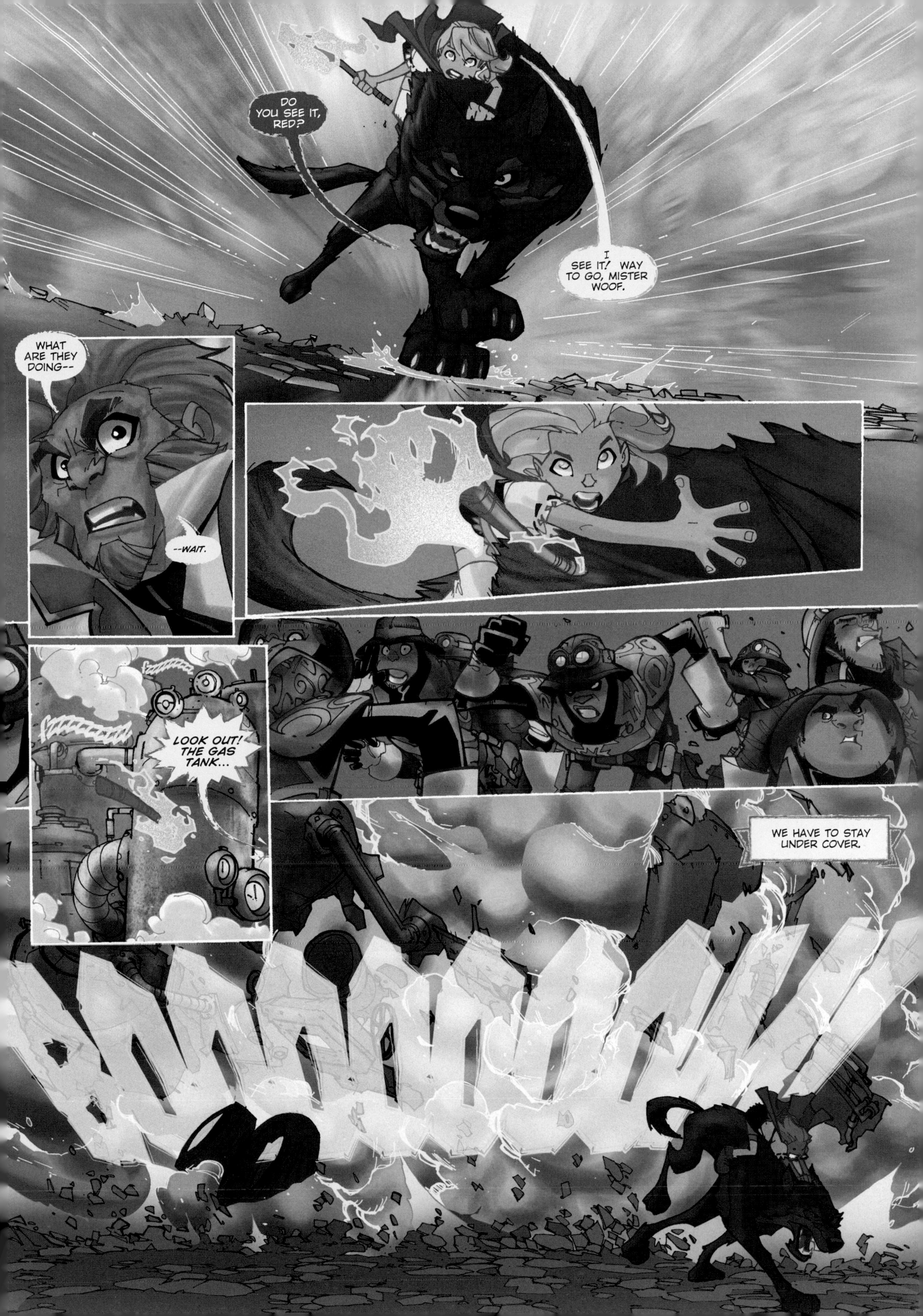

DO YOU SEE IT, RED?
I SEE IT! WAY TO GO, MISTER WOOF.
WHAT ARE THEY DOING--
--WAIT.
LOOK OUT! THE GAS TANK...
WE HAVE TO STAY UNDER COVER.

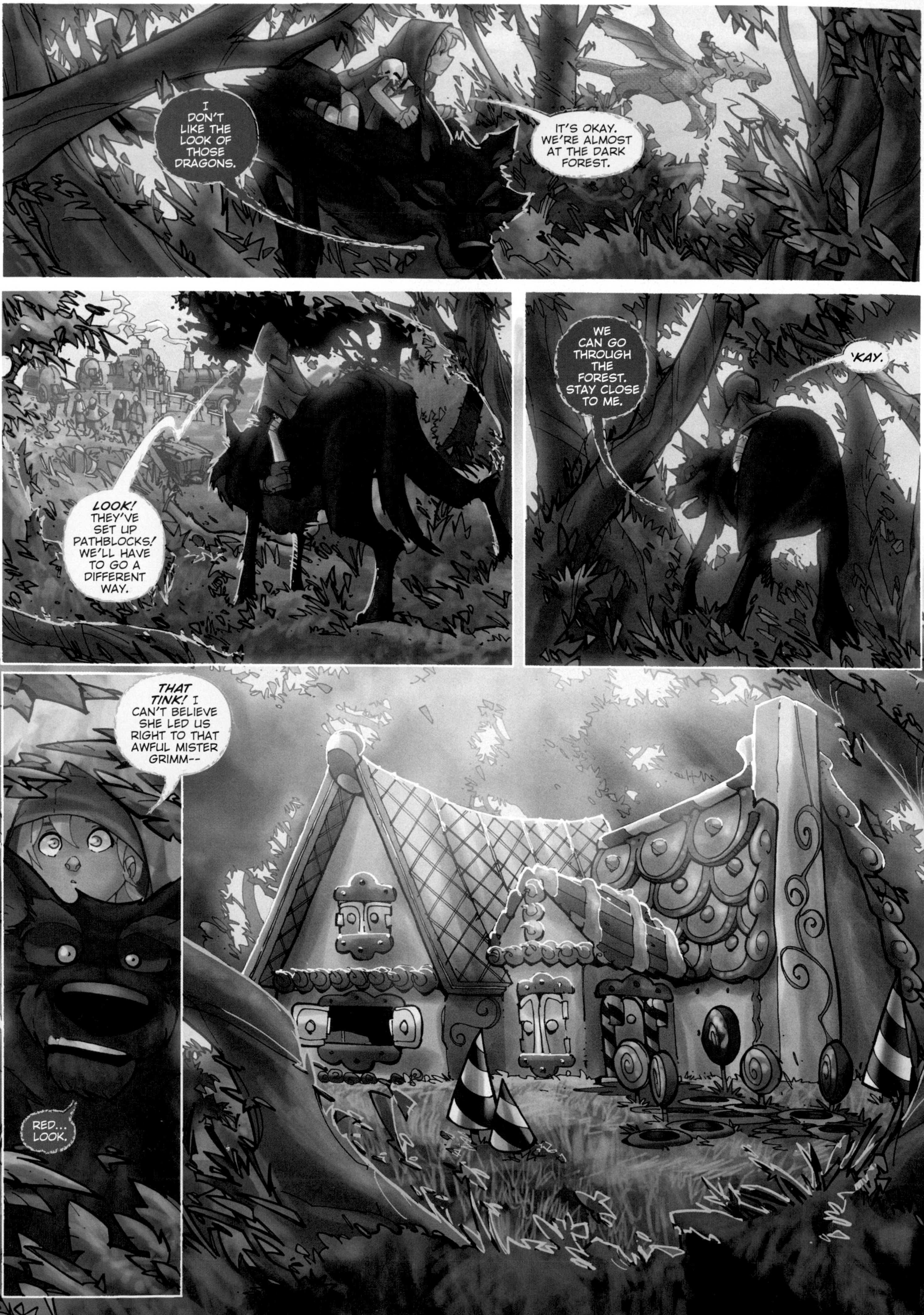
I DON'T LIKE THE LOOK OF THOSE DRAGONS.
IT'S OKAY. WE'RE ALMOST AT THE DARK FOREST.
LOOK! THEY'VE SET UP PATHBLOCKS! WE'LL HAVE TO GO A DIFFERENT WAY.
WE CAN GO THROUGH THE FOREST. STAY CLOSE TO ME.
'KAY.
THAT TINK! I CAN'T BELIEVE SHE LED US RIGHT TO THAT AWFUL MISTER GRIMM--
RED... LOOK.

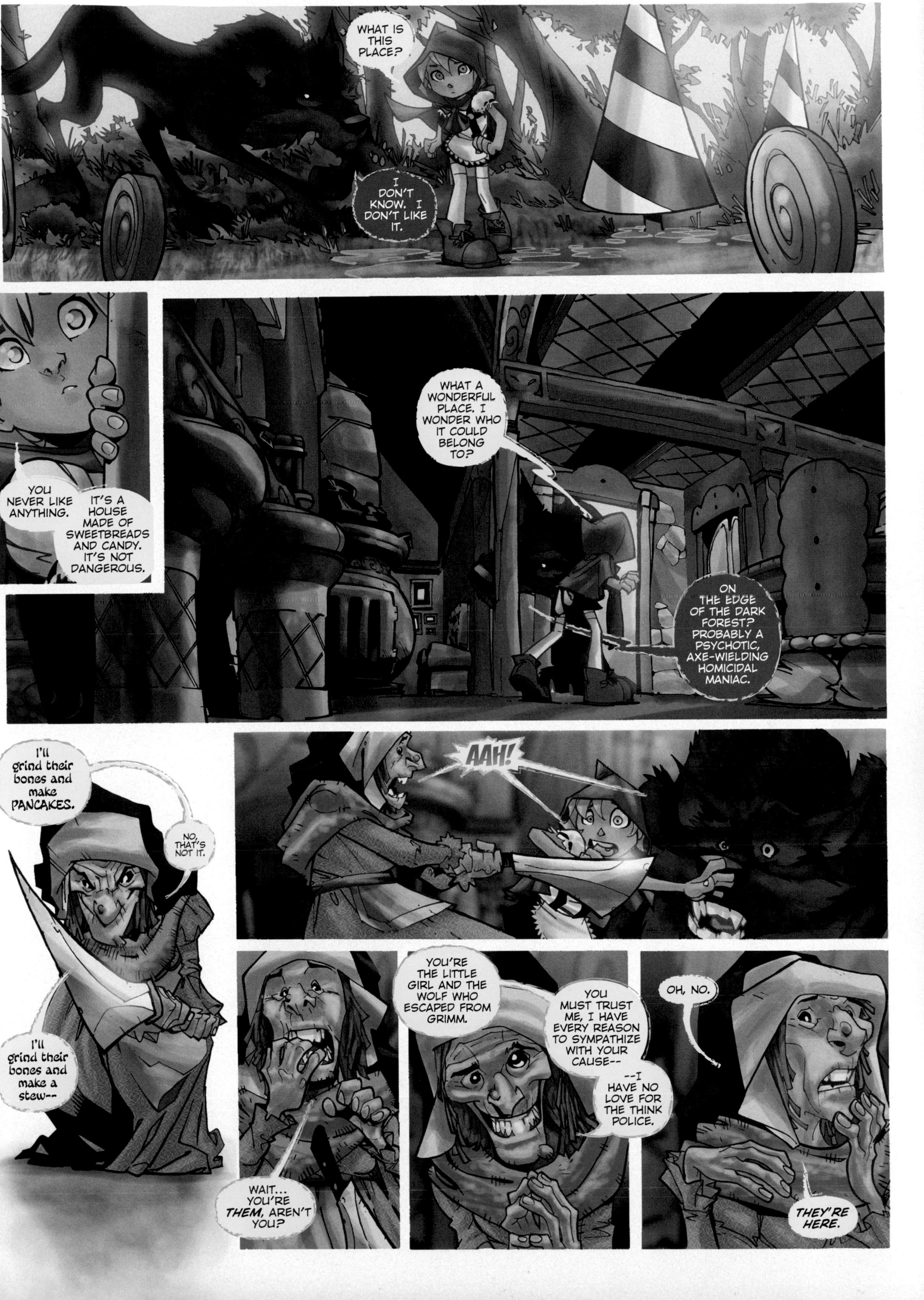
WHAT IS THIS PLACE?
I DON'T KNOW. I DON'T LIKE IT.
YOU NEVER LIKE ANYTHING.
IT'S A HOUSE MADE OF SWEETBREADS AND CANDY. IT'S NOT DANGEROUS.
WHAT A WONDERFUL PLACE. I WONDER WHO IT COULD BELONG TO?
ON THE EDGE OF THE DARK FOREST? PROBABLY A PSYCHOTIC, AXE-WIELDING HOMICIDAL MANIAC.
I'll grind their bones and make PANCAKES.
NO, THAT'S NOT IT.
I'll grind their bones and make a stew--
AAH!
WAIT... YOU'RE *THEM*, AREN'T YOU?
YOU'RE THE LITTLE GIRL AND THE WOLF WHO ESCAPED FROM GRIMM.
YOU MUST TRUST ME, I HAVE EVERY REASON TO SYMPATHIZE WITH YOUR CAUSE--
--I HAVE NO LOVE FOR THE THINK POLICE.
OH, NO.
THEY'RE HERE.

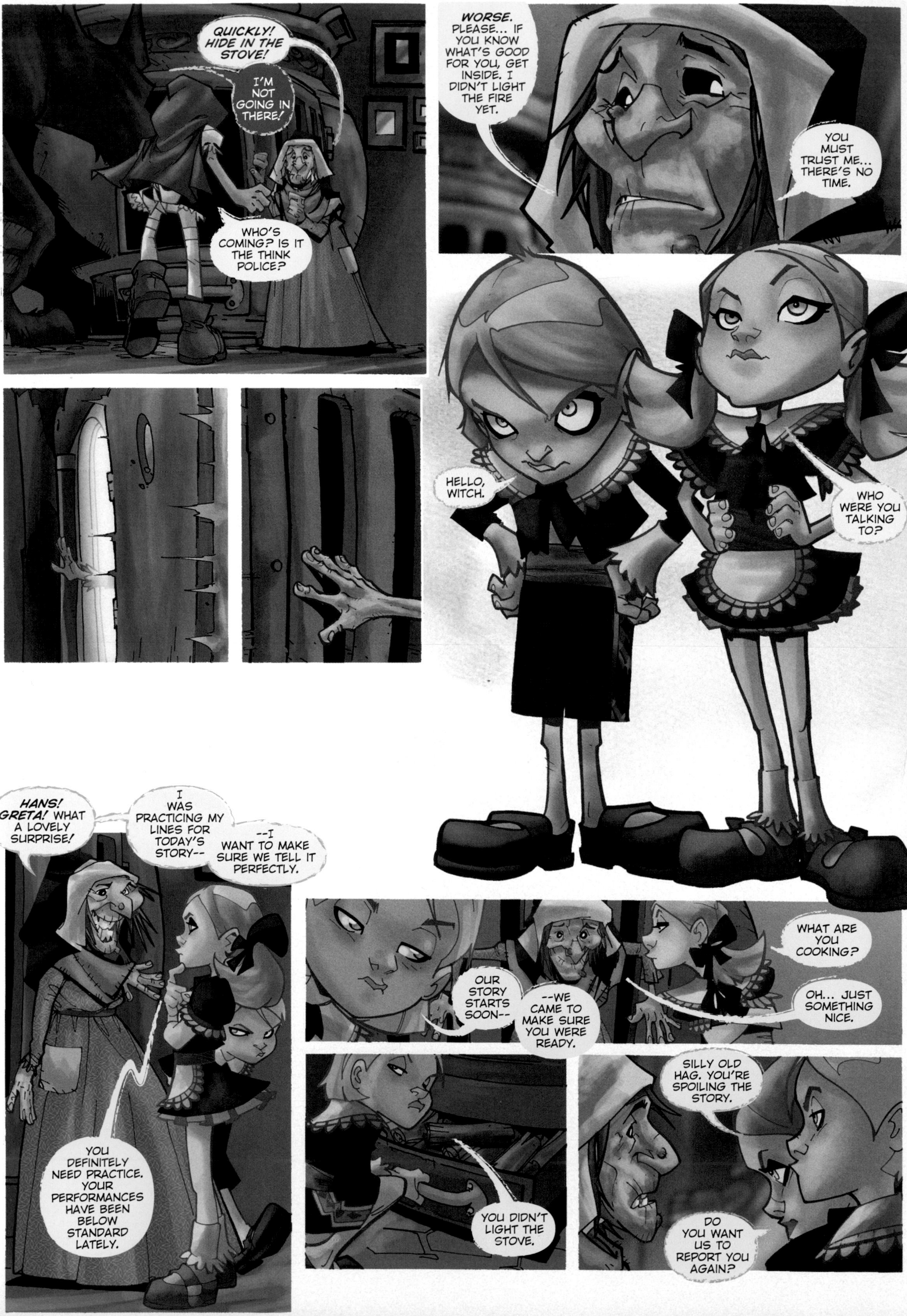
QUICKLY! HIDE IN THE STOVE!
I'M NOT GOING IN THERE!
WHO'S COMING? IS IT THE THINK POLICE?
WORSE. PLEASE... IF YOU KNOW WHAT'S GOOD FOR YOU, GET INSIDE. I DIDN'T LIGHT THE FIRE YET.
YOU MUST TRUST ME... THERE'S NO TIME.
HELLO, WITCH.
WHO WERE YOU TALKING TO?
HANS! GRETA! WHAT A LOVELY SURPRISE!
I WAS PRACTICING MY LINES FOR TODAY'S STORY--
--I WANT TO MAKE SURE WE TELL IT PERFECTLY.
YOU DEFINITELY NEED PRACTICE. YOUR PERFORMANCES HAVE BEEN BELOW STANDARD LATELY.
WHAT ARE YOU COOKING?
OUR STORY STARTS SOON--
--WE CAME TO MAKE SURE YOU WERE READY.
OH... JUST SOMETHING NICE.
YOU DIDN'T LIGHT THE STOVE.
SILLY OLD HAG. YOU'RE SPOILING THE STORY.
DO YOU WANT US TO REPORT YOU AGAIN?

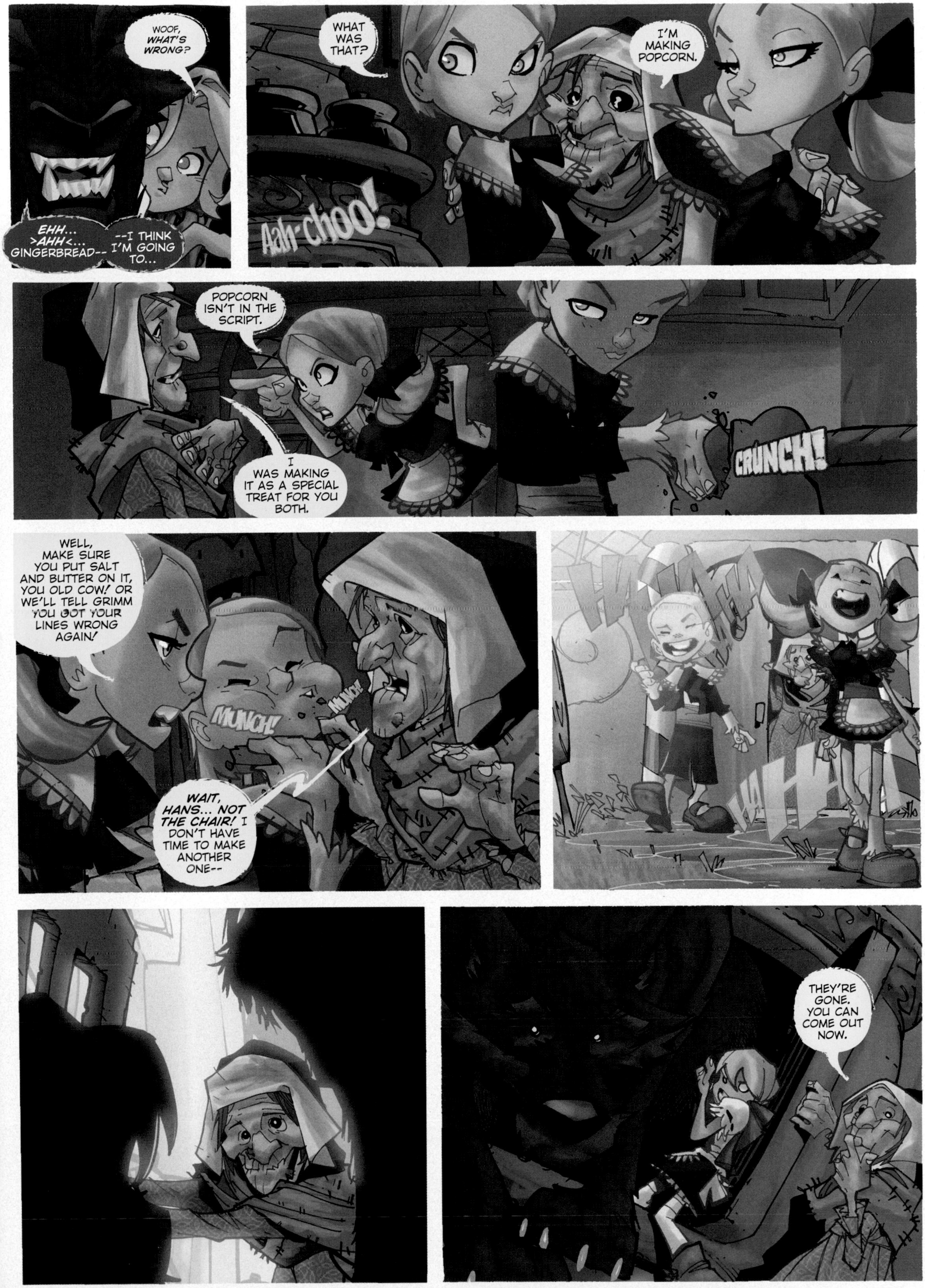
WOOF, WHAT'S WRONG?
EHH... >AHH<... GINGERBREAD--
--I THINK I'M GOING TO...
WHAT WAS THAT?
I'M MAKING POPCORN.
Aah-choo!
POPCORN ISN'T IN THE SCRIPT.
I WAS MAKING IT AS A SPECIAL TREAT FOR YOU BOTH.
CRUNCH!
WELL, MAKE SURE YOU PUT SALT AND BUTTER ON IT, YOU OLD COW! OR WE'LL TELL GRIMM YOU GOT YOUR LINES WRONG AGAIN!
MUNCH!
MUNCH!
WAIT, HANS... NOT THE CHAIR! I DON'T HAVE TIME TO MAKE ANOTHER ONE--
THEY'RE GONE. YOU CAN COME OUT NOW.

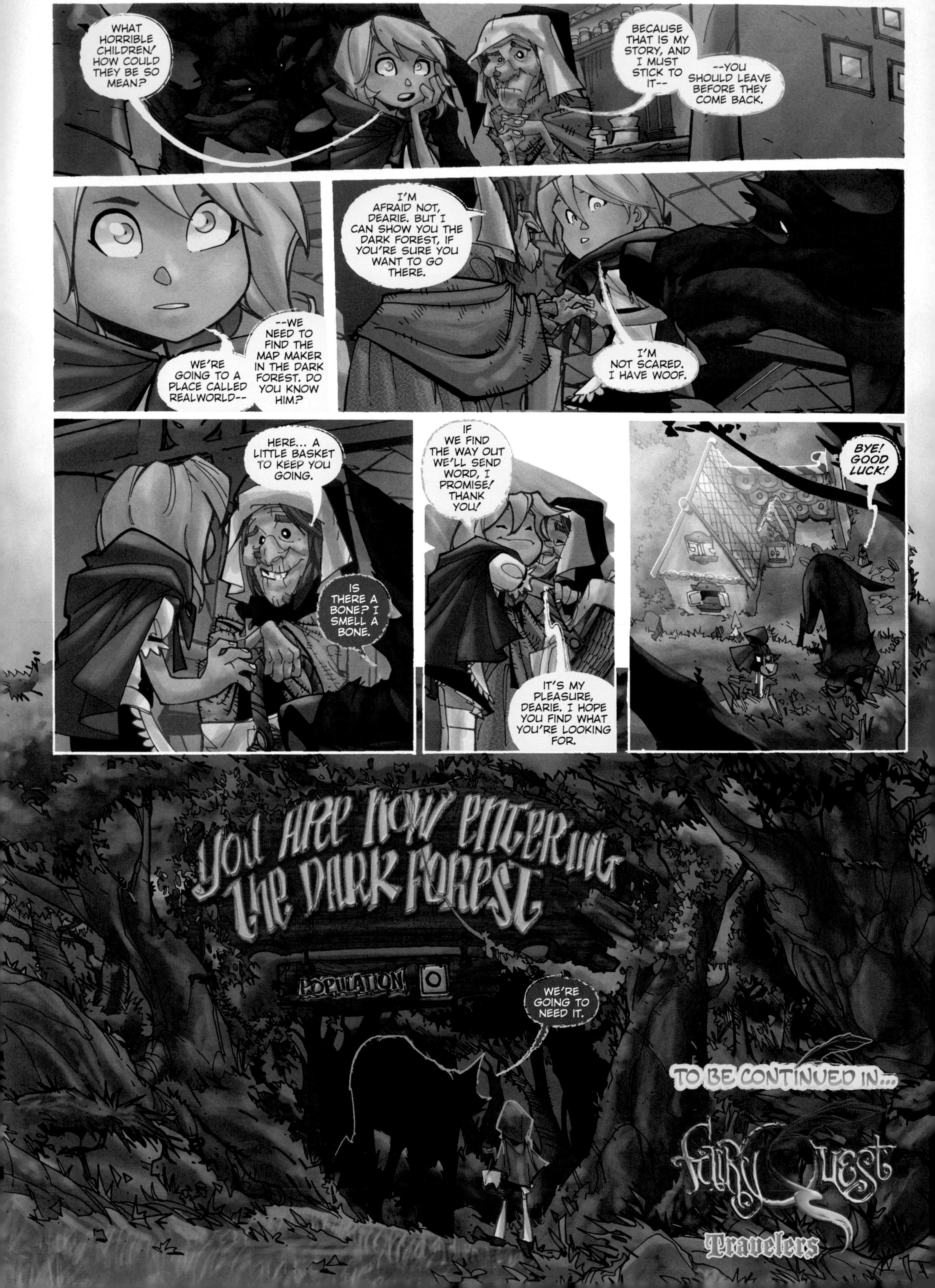
WHAT HORRIBLE CHILDREN! HOW COULD THEY BE SO MEAN?
BECAUSE THAT IS MY STORY, AND I MUST STICK TO IT--
--YOU SHOULD LEAVE BEFORE THEY COME BACK.
WE'RE GOING TO A PLACE CALLED REALWORLD--
--WE NEED TO FIND THE MAP MAKER IN THE DARK FOREST. DO YOU KNOW HIM?
I'M AFRAID NOT, DEARIE. BUT I CAN SHOW YOU THE DARK FOREST, IF YOU'RE SURE YOU WANT TO GO THERE.
I'M NOT SCARED. I HAVE WOOF.
HERE... A LITTLE BASKET TO KEEP YOU GOING.
IS THERE A BONE? I SMELL A BONE.
IF WE FIND THE WAY OUT WE'LL SEND WORD, I PROMISE! THANK YOU!
IT'S MY PLEASURE, DEARIE. I HOPE YOU FIND WHAT YOU'RE LOOKING FOR.
BYE! GOOD LUCK!
YOU ARE NOW ENTERING THE DARK FOREST
POPULATION 0
WE'RE GOING TO NEED IT.
TO BE CONTINUED IN...
Fairy Quest
Travelers

Art Gallery

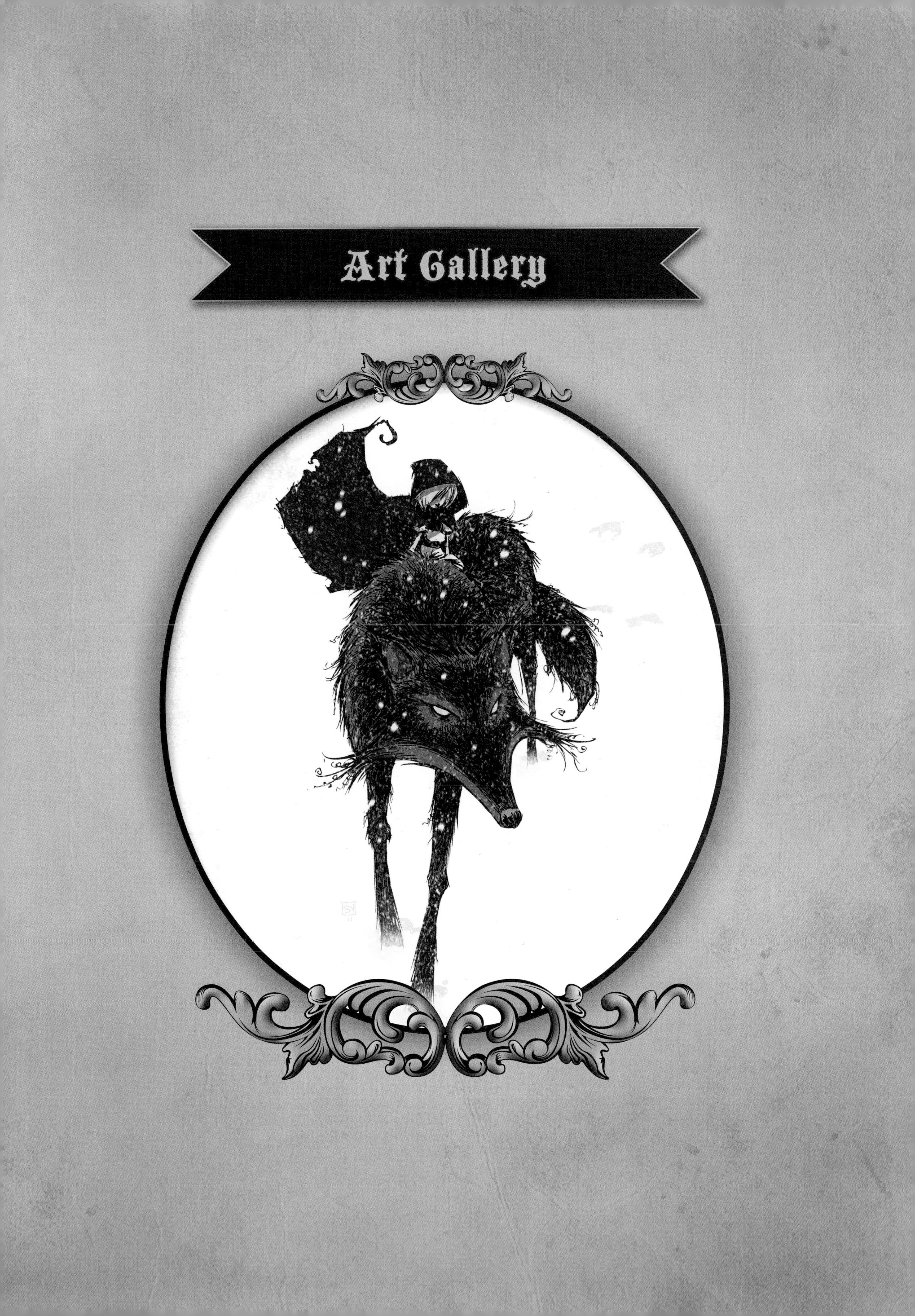

HUMBERTO RAMOS
COLORS BY LEONARDO OLEA

Covers

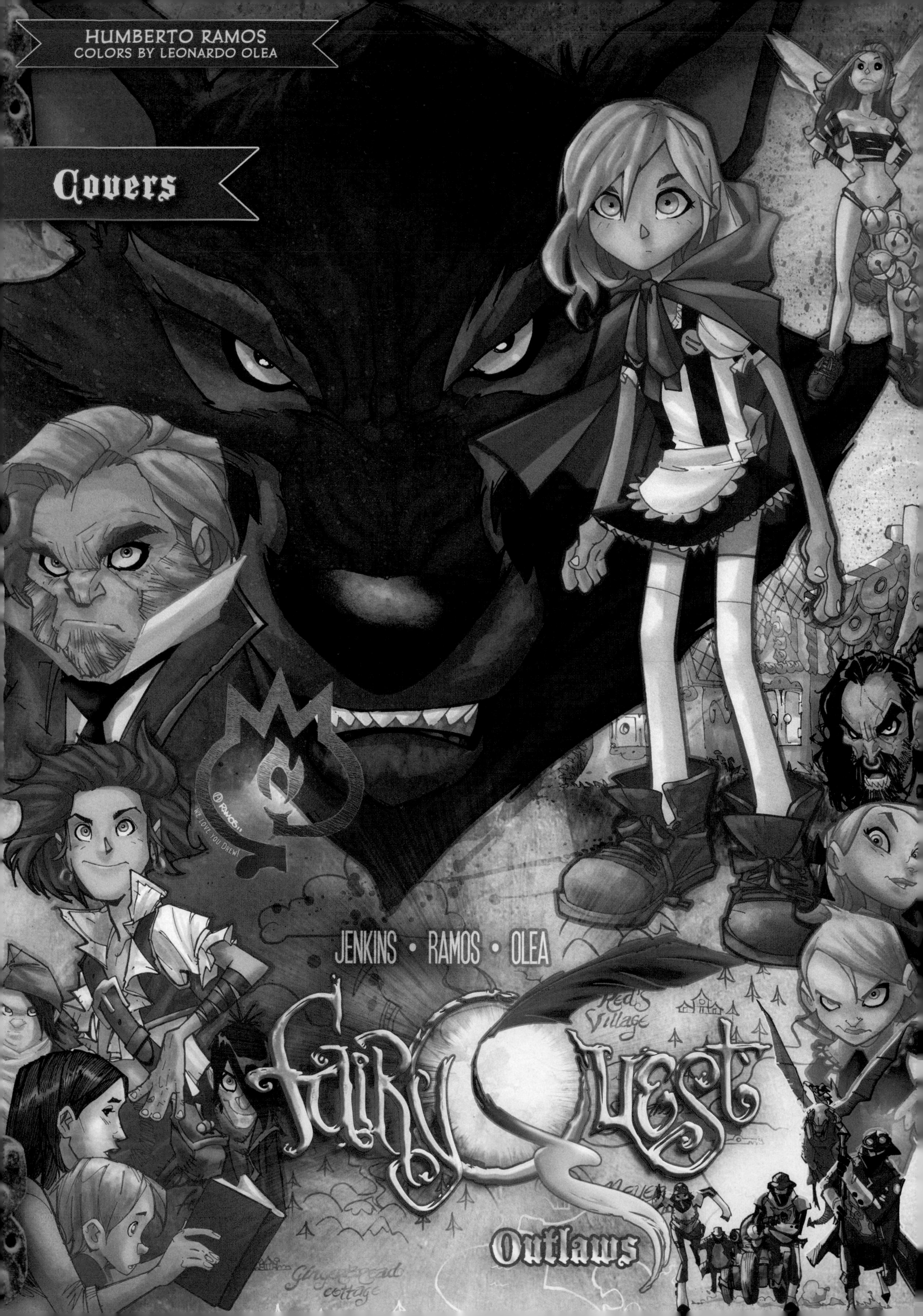
JENKINS • RAMOS • OLEA
FairyQuest
Outlaws
Red's Village
Gingerbread cottage
WE LOVE YOU DREW!

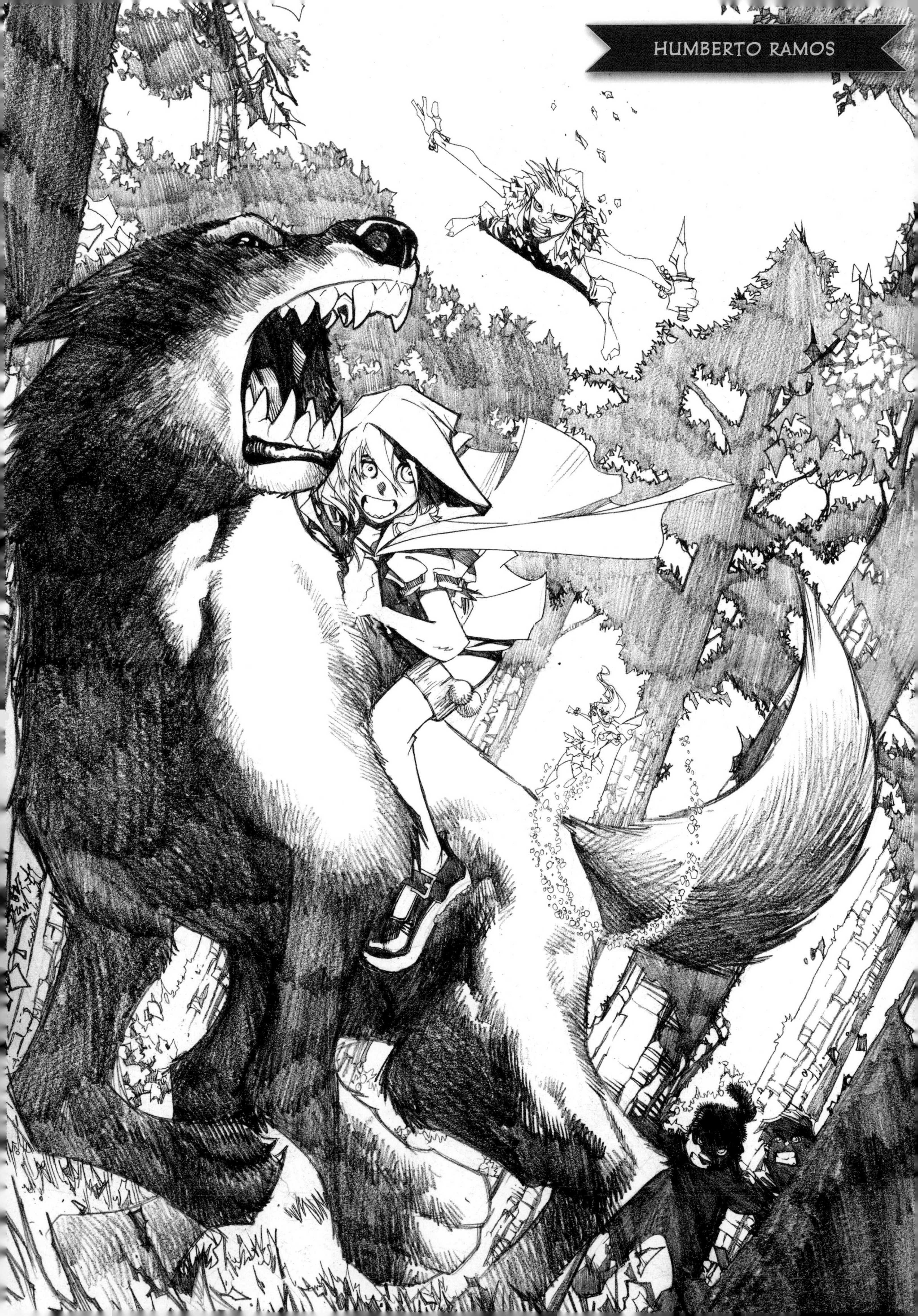
HUMBERTO RAMOS

HUMBERTO RAMOS
COLORS BY LEONARDO OLEA

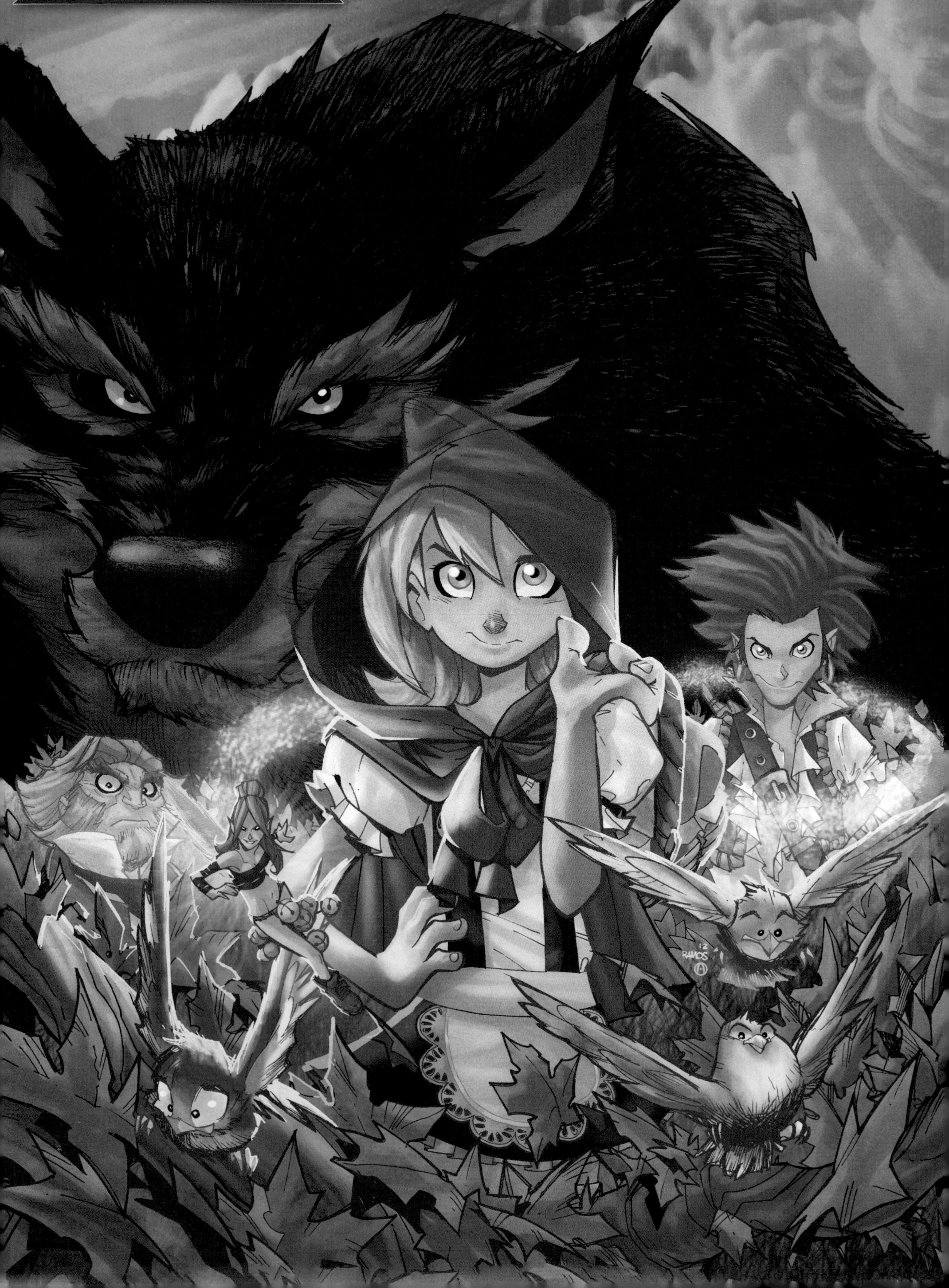
'12
RAMOS

Pin-Ups

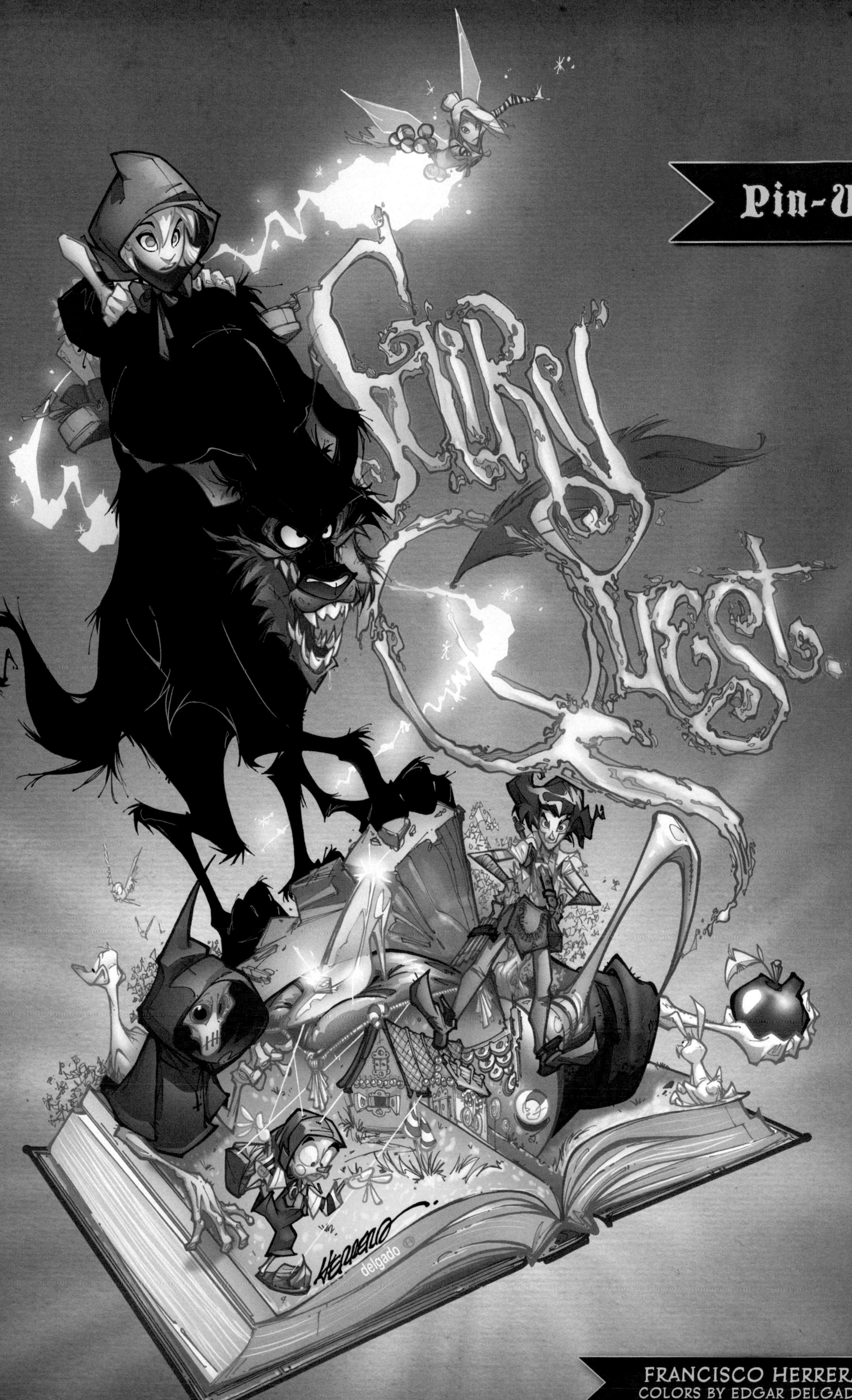
Fairy Quest.

FRANCISCO HERRERA
COLORS BY EDGAR DELGADO

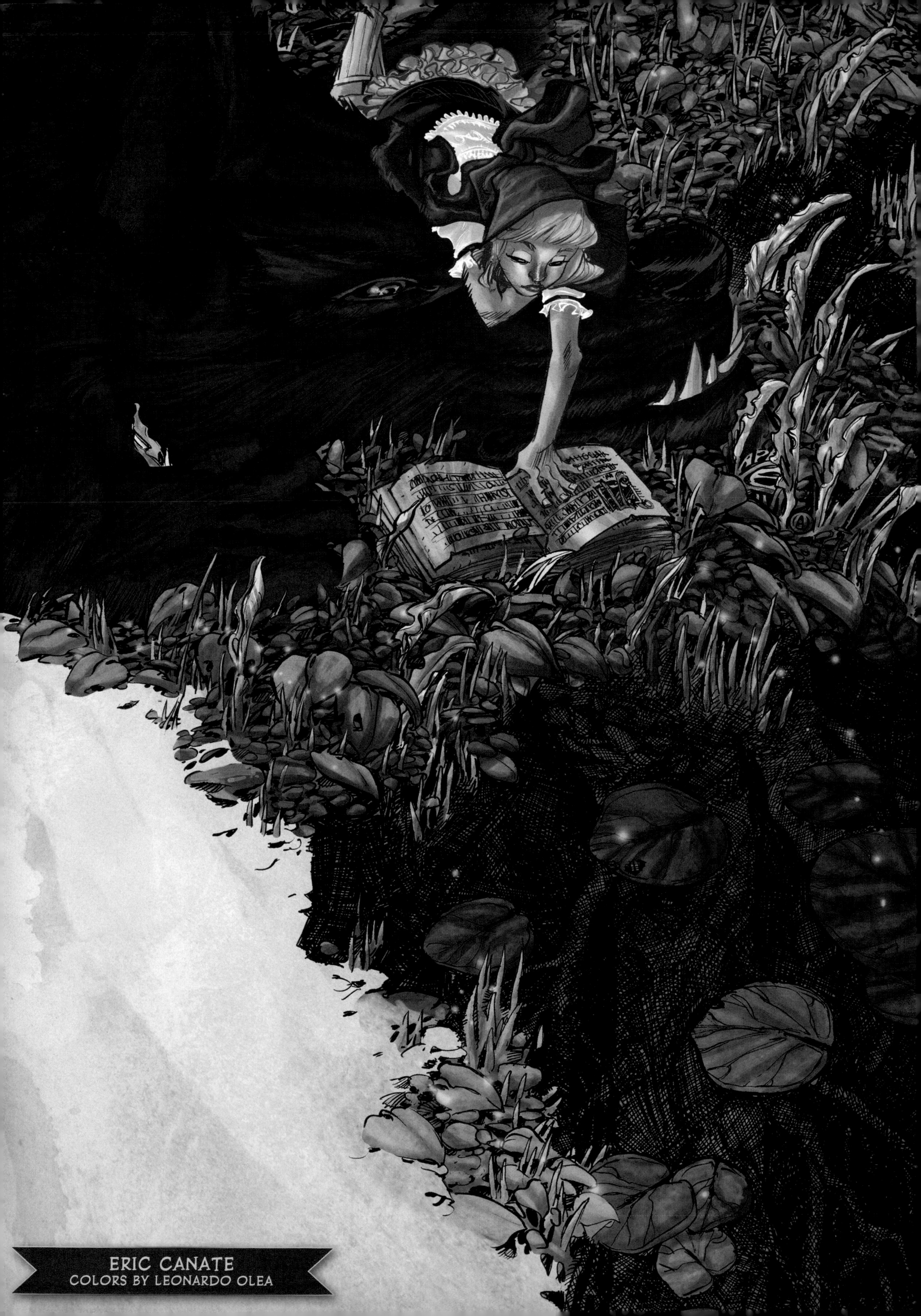

ERIC CANATE
COLORS BY LEONARDO OLEA

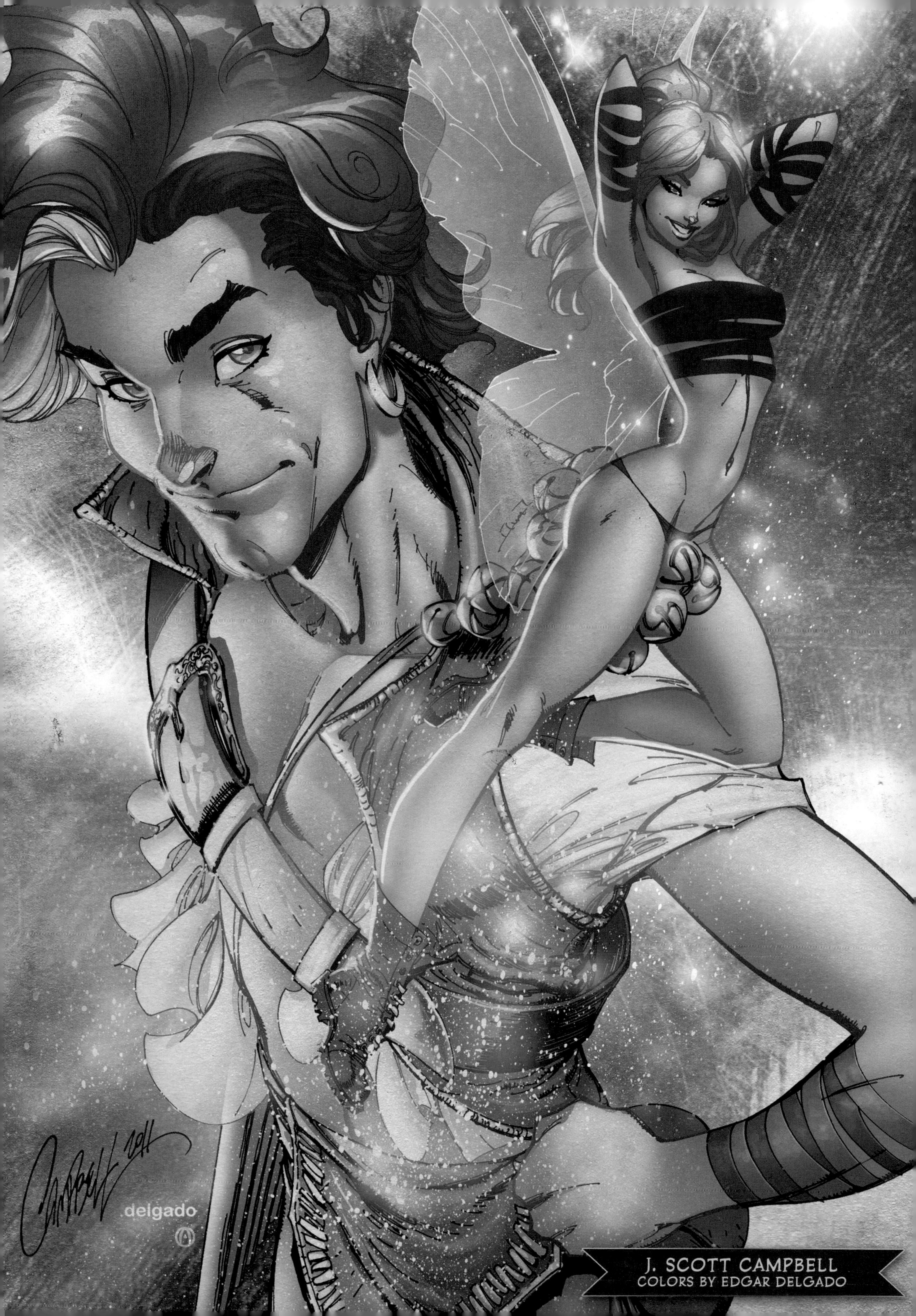
delgado
J. SCOTT CAMPBELL
COLORS BY EDGAR DELGADO

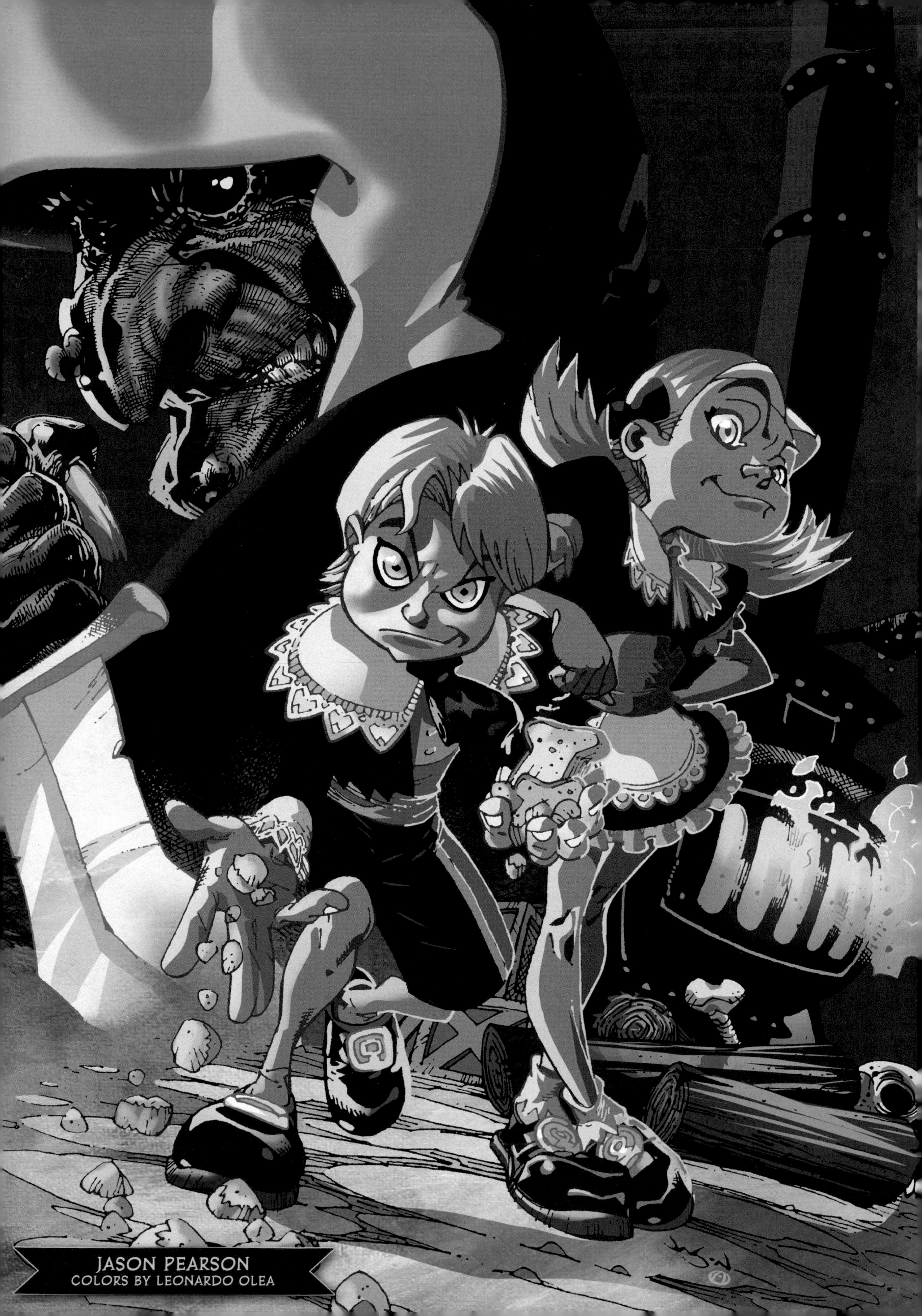
JASON PEARSON
COLORS BY LEONARDO OLEA